# RACE AND COLOUR
## IN
## CARIBBEAN LITERATURE

# RACE AND COLOUR
# IN
# CARIBBEAN LITERATURE

## G. R. COULTHARD

Senior Lecturer in Spanish Language and Literature
in the University of the West Indies

*Issued under the auspices of the*
*Institute of Race Relations*

OXFORD UNIVERSITY PRESS
LONDON   NEW YORK   TORONTO
1962

*Oxford University Press, Amen House, London, E.C.4*

GLASGOW NEW YORK TORONTO MELBOURNE WELLINGTON
BOMBAY CALCUTTA MADRAS KARACHI LAHORE DACCA
CAPE TOWN SALISBURY NAIROBI IBADAN ACCRA
KUALA LUMPUR HONG KONG

First published in 1958 by the Escuela de Estudios Hispano-Americanos de Sevilla, under the title *Raza y Color en la Literatura Antillana*.

English Translation
© Institute of Race Relations, 1962

PRINTED IN GREAT BRITAIN

# CONTENTS

# INTRODUCTION

THIS book is essentially a literary study, that is to say that the theme of race and colour is dealt with as it appears in the imaginative literature of the West Indies. This does not mean that the analysis of the theme of race and colour in terms of literary subjects is not closely linked with other aspects of Caribbean life—social, political, cultural and psychological—which it may serve to illuminate and explain.

The literature of independent Latin America, including the French-speaking island of Haiti, was born in the early nineteenth century amid the clamour of the struggle for independence from Spain and, as might be expected, a great part of this literature was of an essentially political nature. The subsequent history of the independent republics during the rest of the nineteenth century, and indeed up to the present day, has been that of a series of more or less violent political struggles which have broken out periodically and which have found expression in civil strife of varying degrees of magnitude. Under such conditions it is not surprising that writers, many of them public figures, should have directed their attention to the social and political reality which surrounded them, which was the cause of much of the unrest and in which many were actively involved. The particularly *engagé* nature of Latin American literature has struck most critics and historians of Latin American culture. So it is that we find the Uruguayan critic, Enrique Rodó, uttering in 1899 the following generalisation about nineteenth-century Latin American poetry:

'Besides, every manifestation of poetry has been more or less subjugated to the supreme necessity of propaganda and action. Art, indeed, has been little more than a heightened form of propaganda.'[1] This assertion comes from an article attacking the prosaic and utilitarian nature of Latin American culture in the nineteenth century, in which Rodó is advocating a more purely aesthetic orientation and, although not completely true, it can stand as a fairly correct assessment of Latin American culture in the period under consideration.

More than fifty years later, one of the most outstanding of Latin American critics, the Cuban, José Antonio Portuondo, writes along similar lines, although in a very different spirit:

> The dominant characteristic of the Latin American novel is not the absorbing presence of nature, but a concern with social matters, the critical outlook manifest in many works, their instrumental function in the historical process of the respective nations. The novel has always been for us an accusatory document, a display of doctrinal propaganda, a calling of attention to serious and urgent social problems so that the mass of readers can take immediate action.[2]

Rodó adopts a critical attitude to the predominantly functional nature of Latin American literature and is advocating greater concern with the art of writing, and in the article quoted from is dealing with the poet Rubén Darío, who had headed a revolt against utilitarian, propagandising literature. Darío, in fact, in the introduction to his *Prosas profanas* (1895), had declared the repugnance he felt for the contemporary world and his love of Ancient Greece, the Roman Empire at the time of its decadence, and the refinement and aristocratic elegance of the eighteenth-century French court. All that interested him in America was the 'sensual Inca on his golden throne', clearly imagining the court of the Incas in terms of the courts of Rome and France. Portuondo on the other hand not only believes that the main characteristic of Latin American culture historically has been militant, but that this tradition, which has its beginnings during the war of independence against Spain, is the *right* tradition and that writers should perpetuate it. In this connexion it is perhaps not without significance that Rubén Darío, the champion of aestheticism, by 1905 in his *Cantos de vida y esperanza* should have abandoned his ivory tower to write in virile and aggressive tones in favour of the spiritual and political independence of Latin America, in the face of North American political and cultural incursions. His last major work, indeed, is a poem on the future of the Argentine Republic, which he sees as a melting-pot of all races, bound together by Hispanic cultural values. The aesthetic revolt which he headed was short-lived, covering the period roughly from 1890 to 1910. The reaction brought back American subject matter in the form of essentially American social and political problems. The legacy of Modernism, as the aesthetic movement came to be called, was an increased awareness of the necessity of competent writing, but this new consciousness of style was applied to the serious and urgent problems of Latin American life.

I have insisted on this point because on it depends a generalisation which is fundamental to the present study, namely that up to the present a great deal of Latin American literature has been a literature of themes or of subjects, and any study of this literature over the last 150 years has had inevitably to take this fact into account.

There are, of course, noteworthy exceptions to this generalisation. Recently such writers as the Chilean, Pablo Neruda, the Argentinian, Jorge Luis Borges and, in the nineteenth century, Rubén Darío and José Asunción Silva, have made substantial contributions to the history of Spanish stylistics. Generally speaking, however, style has been subordinated to content and aesthetic considerations sacrificed to the urgency of stating pressing problems, usually of a social or political nature and which demand an immediate solution. Critics too have followed this lead and given importance to certain works because they are social documents, without worrying too much about their literary quality. However much one may deplore this in a cultural situation where the writers themselves consciously lay so much emphasis on the importance of the subject (the 'novel of the jungle', the 'novel of the land', the 'Indian novel', the 'Gaucho novel', the 'novel of the Mexican civil war' are significant labels in this context) it is hardly surprising that the literary historian should feel tempted to examine and analyse precisely what these themes are and how they are handled.[3]

From the beginnings of Latin American literature the use of certain subjects, human types and local settings has been recommended by political thinkers and authors alike. The opinions and literary proclamations of such writers as Andrés Bello, Domingo Faustino Sarmiento, Bartolomé Mitre are too well known to be quoted here. But the fact remains that throughout the nineteenth century the need to build a national culture and a national literature in each republic has been stated with monotonous regularity. And the way to achieve this end was by using local subjects, dealing with local problems. This current has run, uninterrupted except for the brief twenty years' hiatus of Modernism, down to the present day. But after Modernism writers returned to the analysis and interpretation of their society, more conscious of literary techniques, but more than ever bent on finding out the truth about themselves and their countries and stating it to the world. The tradition of localism, or Americanism as it has often been called, has been attacked and criticised by some writers who do not feel comfortable under the imposition of local themes as a sort of cultural duty. One of the most effective protests against literary nationalism and the tyranny of local colour comes from the Argentine writer Jorge Luis Borges, who states the problem pointedly and with humour in the following passage from one of his essays:

> Gibbon observes that the Arab book *par excellence* is the Koran. There are no camels, and I believe that if there were any doubt as to the authenticity of the Koran this absence of camels would be sufficient proof that it is an Arab book. It was written by Mohammed and Mohammed as an Arab had no reason for thinking that camels are an essential part of the Arab world. For him they were merely part of the everyday reality and he felt no need to emphasize their presence. On the other hand a fake, a tourist or an Arab nationalist would have abounded in camels; he would have had masses of camels, caravans of camels on every page; but Mohammed as an Arab was not concerned with this. He knew it was possible to be an Arab without camels. And I believe that we Argentinians can be like Mohammed; we can believe in the possibility of being Argentinians without an abundance of local colour.[4]

However, up to the present Borges's attitude has been a minority attitude and, for good or for evil, the major current of Latin American culture has followed a channel of localism and nationalism.

It may appear to the reader that we have made a long preamble before arriving at a statement of the problem of Caribbean literature, but this is because Caribbean culture as a whole has had a cultural development very similar to that of continental Latin America. We find, for example, that Haiti, which achieved independence before the Spanish American colonies and was born into a different European cultural tradition, has an almost exactly parallel line of development. The British and French territories have not as yet achieved full independence and only started to have a literature of their own in the 1920s. This means that the point of departure of their literature comes almost one hundred years after that of Haiti and the rest of Latin America. Nevertheless, their cultural process seems more and more to be assuming features typical of Latin American culture-localism as far as subject matter is concerned: local settings and human types, and the use of dialect in more or less modified forms. Even the characteristic Latin American dispute between the writer's or artist's claim to interpret the reality of his own country at the risk of artificiality and affectation, and the universalists who claim the right to pronounce on whatever subject they like, is already a commonplace of British West Indian literary discussion.

Even the most cursory glance at the literature (and the painting, sculpture, music and dancing) of the Caribbean, in Spanish, French or English, reveals a constant concern for what I have called race and colour. *The Negro in Caribbean Literature* might, at first sight, have seemed a more appropriate title for this study, taking the Negro as a collective type, like the gaucho, the Indian, the gringo. However, the subject is too complex and *The Negro in Caribbean Literature* suggests a simplification of a situation which is far from simple. *Race and Colour* on the other hand embraces a diversity of social, cultural and historical relations between the man of colour (Negro or mulatto), who thinks of himself and writes consciously as a coloured man, and the white world. This title also brings in the fact of colour among coloured people and finally includes writing by white authors on subjects connected with the presence of coloured people in most of the Caribbean countries, as for example the anti-slavery novels in Cuba and the Afro-Cuban movement, both concerned with the fact of coloured people in Cuba, although the writers involved in both these trends were, with rare exceptions, white.

Geographically, for purposes of this study, the term 'Caribbean' has been used to mean the islands of the Caribbean Sea, although British and French Guiana have been included. The countries of the Caribbean possess a high degree of historical homogeneity—colonisation by European countries, extinction of the aboriginal peoples, importation of Negroes as slaves from Africa to replace the extinct Indians as a work force, cultivation of sugar and coffee, and finally independence or semi-independence. The Guianas, although continental, are very West Indian in character and in their way of life and also have the same, or similar, racial and historical characteristics.

# CHAPTER I

# THE ANTI-SLAVERY NOVEL IN CUBA:
# INDIANS AND NEGROES

ONE of the aims of writers in Latin America in the nineteenth century was to find an original and distinctive note for their literary creations and one of the subjects they introduced to lend an unmistakable American flavour to their works was the autochthonous Indian. It is a commonplace of Latin American literary criticism that the Indian of the nineteenth century Romantics was idealised and totally artificial. Nevertheless, the quantity of Indianist writing is impressive,[1] and the fact that the Indians of certain countries had died out did not prevent writers in those same countries from using them as a subject of literature. Indeed, curiously enough, it was in the countries which had not had any Indians for years that the best works on the Indian theme were produced, in Uruguay and Santo Domingo.[2] Cuba, another country without Indians, was not far behind with its mid-nineteenth century *siboneista* school. As much as in continental America, writers of the Spanish Caribbean islands aimed at producing a literature of strikingly national character, and their hankering after a literature possessing distinctive American features found its solution in the equation Indian plus landscape.[3] There is no doubt that the enthusiasm for Indian subjects and historical figures, even in countries where the Indian had ceased to exist as was the case in the Caribbean, had its roots in anti-Spanish sentiment. The characteristics of romantic Indianism are an idealisation of the Indian and vilification of the Spaniards: Indian heroes and Spanish villains. Very often writers would go back to the world of the Indian before the Conquest and depict him as living in a sort of golden age, simple, primitive and ingenuous in his tropical paradise. The Spaniard is seen to burst into this highly idealised Caribbean Arcadia—cruel, treacherous, lusting for power and wealth. The following vision of the Indian living the life of the Noble Savage, by the Dominican poet Salomé Ureña de Henríquez, is very typical:

> Land of enchantment
> orchard of love
> which preserves the charms
> of the first Eden.
> In its pleasant fields
> it was able to enjoy
> in its simple existence
> a life of peace.
> The Indian family
> the race of Quisqueya
> in happy possession
> of its fair land
> in its innocence
> watched life flow calmly
> no sorrow in its soul,
> no yoke on its neck.
> The woods gave free
> their fruits in abundance,
> the hills their flowers,
> the rivers their waters;
> and generous, fertile,
> the depths of the seas
> gave fish in thousands
> a rich storehouse.[4]

This happy and simple existence is shattered by the arrival of the Spaniards, and the following portrait of the Spanish commander Ojeda is a stereotype of the way the Spaniards were depicted:

> Ojeda, the iron-souled Spaniard
> deep-souled fanatic,
> daring and fortunate adventurer,
> diabolical in his wiles.[5]

In the same poem we find applied to the Spaniards such epithets as 'ferocious foreigner', 'the vile rabble', 'bloody tigers', and the Spanish victory over the Indians is described as due to 'perfidy' and 'treachery'. Another such work, by the Dominican Manuel de Jesús Galván is *Enriquillo* (1882). This novel has many features in common with Salomé Ureña de Henríquez's *Anacaona*; the hero is an Indian chief Enriquillo, who has been baptised and is a man of high ideals. He is, however, driven to resist the Spaniards as a result of their treachery and bad faith. The tone of the book is less stridently anti-Spanish, that is to say, not *all* the Spaniards are depicted as villains, and the happy ending to the novel is brought about by the concession by the Spanish authorities of a section of the island where Enriquillo can lead his own life as chief of his own people. This concession is due to 'the magnanimity and sense of justice of a great Monarch and the abnegation and patience of an honorable Spanish soldier'.[6]

It would not be pertinent to this study to enter in detail into a discussion of the copious Indianist literature written in the Spanish Caribbean. It is none the less important to emphasise its main characteristics and to indicate its significance, for the use of the Indian theme in Latin American literature was much more than a question of local colour and exoticism. It amounted, in the first place, to an identification of the free and independent Latin Americans of the ex-Spanish colonies with the original, pre-Conquest inhabitants of the new republics. It was the affirmation of a non-Spanish past. This identification, brought about through poems and novels, could be regarded as something purely artificial and gratuitous, since the romantic Indian is completely lacking in reality and corresponds in psychology and behaviour to no American Indian, either in the past or the present. Nevertheless, this idealised, artificial Indian played an important part in the formation of a national feeling in the new republics. Readers of poems and novels were drawn into a spiritual and emotional identification with their American ancestors, ancestors not necessarily in the racial sense, but ancestors on the same land. There is no doubt that the Mexican, Argentinian, Dominican or Cuban reader of Indianist novels and poems in nineteenth-century Latin America, felt himself Indian when he read of the sufferings of the Indians, of their bitter and heroic struggle to defend their land and their dignity against the cruel, grasping Spaniards, who were endeavouring to take their lands and to enslave them. From this point of view, literary Indianism made an important contribution to national and patriotic integration as it provided the peoples of the new republics with an emotional link with the past and with the past inhabitants of their countries.

In Cuba, which remained a Spanish colony until 1898, Indianism served the double purpose of cementing national feeling and of protesting in a veiled manner against the Spanish occupation of Cuba, since direct criticism of Spain was not tolerated.

The connexion between literary Indianism, emotional and sentimental, and the development of political feeling in Latin America is well illustrated by the following statement by Max Henríquez Ureña:

> Indianist literature appears in the Dominican Republic after the brief re-annexation by Spain which took place in 1861. Before that the patriotic subject was that of the Virgins of Galindo in face of Haitian invasion, celebrated by Del Monte, to remind us of the horrors of the long captivity under the flag of Haiti. The fact of the re-annexation brought the Dominican face to face with Spain for the first time. It was the war of national restoration, fought against Spain, which moved Dominicans to remember the vanished Indians and to weep over their misfortunes.[7]

In the second place, from a purely literary point of view, the Latin American Romantics were following a tendency traced by European Romanticism, in seeking to create a literature with distinctively national subject matter and the American Indian had all the prerequisites to fill such a role. It is also obvious that this desire to have a national literature, with subjects different from those used in European literature, was not purely literary, but corresponded to a basically political attitude of patriotic and separatist affirmation.[8]

This abundant literature on Indian subjects, as has been pointed out, has its roots in psychological and political reality. But in the physical contemporary reality of the Caribbean islands it had no basis at all. Statistics for the population of Latin America (as provided in Angel Rosenblat's book *The Development of the Indigenous Population in America*[9] show no figure for the Indian population of the Caribbean islands in 1825. On the other hand, there is an impressive figure for Negroes: 1,960,000 out of a total population of 2,843,000 and out of the non-Negro population, 401,000 are given as 'mulattos and mixed' (*mestizos*). The figure for whites is 482,000. This means that at the beginning of the period under study there was a population of 2,361,000 Negroes and mulattos as against a white population of 482,000. There were no Indians.

The Negro was not completely ignored, but appeared in a very different kind of literature from that in which we have seen the idealised Indian. It was in fact a literature produced in Cuba by liberal intellectuals dissatisfied with the Spanish colonial regime.

The first work of this type was the novel *Francisco: The Plantation*, or *The Delights of Country Life*, written by Anselmo Suárez Romero in 1839 but not published until 1880 in New York. The book was written by Suárez Romero on the suggestion of Domingo del Monte with the object of offering a realistic picture of the slavery situation in Cuba, in order to supply documentary evidence for Dr. Richard R. Madden, British Commissioner on the Mixed Arbitration Tribunal, on matters connected with the slave trade.[10] In spite of using many of the documents supplied to him by Del Monte, Madden did not translate or have published Suárez Romero's novel, although in a letter to Del Monte he had praised the book, saying: 'I find in this little work, *El Ingenio,* many minute details of description, a correct and precise gift of observation, a rectitude of principles and feelings which I have rarely seen surpassed.'[11] The idea of *Francisco* as an anti-slavery novel was born in the literary meetings held in Del Monte's house, where liberals and supporters of Cuban independence met to discuss the political situation in Cuba. It was clearly originally conceived as a social document, aimed at exhibiting to the world the more repugnant aspects of the institution of slavery and producing the maximum of horror and indignation in the reader.

*Francisco* tells the story of the slave Francisco, who has been punished for seducing a slave-girl belonging to his master's household. By way of punishment he is sent to work on the plantation (he had hitherto occupied the privileged position of coachman to the mistress of the house) and there the son of the slave-holding family, who had himself tried unsuccessfully to seduce the same slave-girl, inflicts on Francisco a life of constant misery and suffering. Finally, to save her lover who is dying from the treatment he is receiving, the girl gives herself to the young master in the hope of mitigating Francisco's sufferings. When he hears of this, Francisco despairs and hangs himself. The novel brings face to face two worlds: that of the masters and that of the slaves. The masters are depicted as demoralised and debased by the institution of slavery, and as incapable of treating the slaves as human beings. Even the mistress of the house, Señora Mendizábal, an otherwise kind and devout woman, is cruel and inhuman with her slaves and the slightest sign of disobedience in a slave immediately makes her become despotic and harsh. When Francisco asks her a second time for permission to marry the girl Dorotea she refuses, largely because she regards it as a weakness to go back on a decision: 'The right government of a house depended for her on the slaves always being wrong and the white people always right.'[12] The other white characters—her son Ricardo, the doctor and the overseer on the estate—are sadistically cruel and take pleasure in torturing and humiliating the slaves. The following passage will serve to give an idea of the scenes of cruelty that abound in the novel:

> Francisco received three hundred and five lashes in the space of ten days, as a result of which he was so weakened that he could not move from his bed for two weeks. The overseer had beaten his buttocks to a pulp of raw flesh and it was a pitiful sight to see them. But he was not satisfied with this, and seeing that Francisco could not go out to work in the fields, he tried every means of harassing him. Among the various ideas suggested to him by his cruelty, none appeared more appropriate than that of rubbing his wounds with dry maize straw soaked in a terrible mixture of brandy, urine, salt and tobacco, until the blood spurted out of the wounds. This was a pleasure, an innocent recreation for Don Antonio, who, laughing loudly, made Francisco let down his trousers, and with his own hands tortured him, not without giving him several blows with his fists and kicks to make him keep still, all the while making crude and obscene jokes. It would be idle to describe the terrible pain suffered by the Negro coachman as he often fainted, only regaining consciousness some hours later. And the overseer, instead of feeling pity at the sight of an almost dying man, laughed and joked all the more and rubbed his wounds with increased vigour.[13]

There are many such passages in *Francisco*, passages to which the reader cannot remain indifferent, and which provoke a strong reaction of anger and hatred for men who are capable of treating their fellow men in such a way. Indeed, Suárez Romero's aim is to bring his readers to a condemnation of the institution of slavery which makes such atrocities possible.

While the attitude of the slave-owning whites stands out in bold outline, the world of the Negro slaves is much vaguer. Francisco is a Negro who had been born in Africa and brought to Cuba as a slave. He is sad and melancholy in temperament partly because he is a slave, but also because he is a man in love but prevented from marrying the object of his love because he is not free to do as he wants. Dorotea is a mulatto, pretty and deli- cate, a slave and frustrated in her love for the same reasons as Francisco. She is capable of sacrifice, since she gives her body to the master, Ricardo, in order to save her lover. Apart from the main characters, there are other Negroes, plantation workers, who are all good, simple people (apart from an overseer who appears to take pleasure in bullying his own people), but they lack any clearly defined character. There are scenes of vivid Afro- Cuban colour in which the author describes the dances and songs of the slaves, as in the following passage:

Always in time to the various rhythms of the drums they would move in a circle, their heads on one side, shaking their arms, the woman following the man, the man following the woman, both face to face, but never touching, never close together. Or they would stand face to face, and circle round, spin rapidly and jump, throwing their bodies backwards. . . .

The drum, for African-born Negroes and also for the Cuban-born Negroes who grow up with them, is a sweeping away, a possession, and when they hear it they feel they are in heaven.

On the songs sung by the Negroes, he writes:

But there are songs which do not change, because they were composed in Africa, and came here with the African-born slaves. The Cuban-born slaves learn them and sing them. They are parents and children, so it should not surprise us. The curious thing is that they never forget them. The slaves come as children, years go by, they grow old and when they can only work as watchmen they sing them alone in their huts, warming themselves at a fire which burns in front of the hut and they remember the land of their fathers, even when they are close to the grave.[14]

These descriptions, written in 1838, are a curious prefiguration of a theme which was to become one of the commonplaces of the Afro-Cuban movement of the period 1920–40, namely the dancing and singing of the Cuban Negro.

Although it was not published until 1880, Suárez Romero's novel was not entirely without effect in as far as its fundamental aim was concerned, for it was read in the literary gatherings at Del Monte's house. Nor was it without literary influence, for the subject and title were taken by another Cuban writer, Mario Zambrana, who published a novel *Francisco The Negro* in 1873, in Santiago, Chile. Its subject, characters, plot and general atmosphere are identical, and it appears that both writers drew their subject from the same source in Cuban life, 'one of many crimes in which slaves were the victims'.[15] Zambrana seems to have heard the story in Del Monte's literary meetings and therefore when invited by some Chilean friends to write a novel on a Cuban subject took as a basis the same 'true story'. In spite of the similarity of the two novels, there are a number of features in Zambrana which are worth emphasising. But first let us see what features they had in common. As in Suárez Romero's novel, there is the confrontation of two worlds, that of the masters and that of the slaves. The white characters, the mistress Josefa de Orellana and her son Carlos, are demoralised by their position as absolute masters; they are harsh and despotic with their slaves. There is also the sadistic overseer who takes pleasure in tormenting the slaves. But the character of the Negro Francisco in Zambrana's novel is well defined and original. He is tough and proud and he hates white people. He even at first hates the mulatto girl Camila, whom he regards as having rejected her race. Zambrana makes no attempt to idealise his Francisco by lending him the feelings and aspirations of a civilised man. He regards the Negroes as barbarians, and he eulogises the primitive life of Africans, refusing to accept that they are better off for having been rescued from primitivism and brought to America.

The civilised man only understands a certain order of ideas and feelings, which are largely artificial and are very weak in those who depend exclusively on nature. As far as the slave is concerned, one should bear in mind the contrast between the idea of civilisation and the rough life of the jungle, and then judge whether the Negro has gained anything in the change. But the Negro loves what you despise: his hidden forest, his coarse music, his primitive customs. Prove to him he is happy, be eloquent and rational with him; but his heart is telling him something very different.[16]

The theme of the primitiveness of the Negro also anticipates a later tendency, for the Afro-Cuban writers were to lay great emphasis on the primitiveness of the Negro, regarding it as a positive quality or seeing in it at least a source of rich material for art and literature. Again, the description Zambrana gives of the mulatto slave-girl Camila, who is otherwise a modest and quiet girl, is of a woman of irresistible sensual attraction. This description, although rather long, is worth quoting, as it contains a eulogy of the beauty and physical attraction of the mulatto, of a type which was in time to become a commonplace all over the Caribbean. It is significant that he makes no mention of her moral attributes since, as he puts it, 'even if she had wished to be the angel of immaculate inspirations, her beauty was not of the kind that inspires pure and spiritual love.'

There was in her something which did not cause a gentle intoxication of the soul, but rather a delirious intoxication of the senses. The graceful curves of her body, the feline grace of her movement, the excited rise and fall of her breasts, her lips made for kissing rather than speech, her voice in whose inflexions was suggested that sweet flexibility which make the caresses of language so passionate; her abundant hair, her figure, possessing the unexpected coiling of the serpent, and above all, her eyes, her black moist and languid eyes which seemed to contain mysterious and passionate secrets: everything made of her the splendid and radiant Venus with whom the body and not the spirit falls in love. Her clothes did not cover any of these charms, but served rather to excite the desire to uncover them. In the atmosphere of this woman there was a poisonous electricity.[17]

These factors, the primitivism of the Negro Francisco and the sensual and voluptuous beauty of the mulatto Camila, are significant as they show in Zambrana a tendency to see in these two coloured figures a character of their own. And it might be added in passing that he gives a brief physical portrait of Francisco whom he describes as an 'ebony Apollo'. All this suggests that Zambrana recognises the existence in Cuba of a separate race living side by side with the white Cubans but possessing its own physical and moral attributes. He also notes the attraction felt by the white man for the beauty of coloured women, and in this he is more subtle than Suárez Romero whose coloured characters have no distinctive racial personality. Suárez Romero was too intent on presenting a revolting picture of the master–slave relationship to notice such things.

Another Cuban novel in which the colour question appears is the novel *Cecilia Valdés*, the first part of which was published in Havana in 1839; the second part was published in 1882 in New York, where its author, Cirilo Villaverde, was living in exile. Villaverde describes his work as 'a novel of Cuban customs' and states in his prologue that his models were Walter Scott, Balzac and Manzoni; his aim was to give 'a description of the customs and passions of a people of flesh and blood, sub-

ject to special political and civil laws, imbued with a certain
order of ideas and surrounded by real and positive influences'.[18]
Villaverde's novel is more complex than the anti-slavery novels
of Suárez Romero and Mario Zambrana, and although its central
theme is not the depiction of the situation of African slaves in
Cuba, it is undeniable that the background of the book is the
colour question in Cuba, and as in Suárez Romero and Zambrana the object of the book is to provoke the indignation of his
readers at the institution of slavery.

Everything that is in the novels of Suárez Romero and Zambrana is to be found in Cecilia Valdés—the sufferings of the slaves
on the plantations, the cruelty and arbitrary behaviour of the
masters and their moral degeneracy as a result of their power of
life and death over the slaves, but there is also an aspect of the
situation which had not been dealt with by the other novelists:
the position of free mulattos in relation to the whites.

The heroine Cecilia is a mulatto, the illegitimate daughter of a
Spanish merchant and a coloured woman of humble origin.
Villaverde does not make of her the sensual half-caste of irresistible sensual attraction we have seen in Zambrana's Francisco.
On the contrary, the portrait Villaverde paints of Cecilia is
almost that of a white woman and her beauty is of a European
type. Indeed, Cecilia would like to pass for white, and it is only
a 'practised eye' that could distinguish non-European features in
her. Another important character is the mulatto José Pimienta,
a free mulatto in love with Cecilia, who resents bitterly the situation of free coloured people in relation to the whites, who enjoy
a far superior degree of social prestige. Cecilia does not love
Pimienta, preferring Leonardo de Gamboa, a white creole. Indeed, she shows a certain snobbish superiority towards other
mulattos. In a telling conversation with another mulatto, Pimienta complains of the whites, saying, 'They take away attractive
coloured girls from us and we dare not even look at white women.'
To which the other mulatto answers: 'If the mulatto girls did
not have a preference for white men, white men would not take
any notice of them.' The attitude of the free mulatto who feels
himself to be the victim of colour prejudice is well brought out
in José Pimienta and other mulatto characters in the book. The
mulatto tailor Uribe answers Pimienta's complaints in the following manner:

What can we do about it, José Dolores? Pretend and keep quiet. Do as the dog does with the wasps; show your teeth so they will think you are laughing. Do you not see that they are the hammer and we the anvil? The whites came first and took the best pieces; we, the coloured ones, came later and we should be thankful they let us gnaw the bones. Take it easy; some day it will be our turn. Things cannot go on for ever like this. Do as I do. Haven't you seen me kiss many hands I would have liked to see cut off? You think I am sincere? Don't you believe it, because the truth is I want nothing to do with white people.[19]

Pimienta suffers because Cecilia has preferred Leonardo, but continues to love her with an impossible love and when Leonardo, who has made Cecilia his mistress, tires of her and decides to marry a woman of his own class and colour, it is Pimienta who stabs him to death at the door of the church where Leonardo is to be married. The inclusion of the psychology of the mulatto constitutes one of the most original features of *Cecilia Valdés*—the resentment at seeing that the whites enjoy privileges from which the mulatto is debarred, and the tendency of the mulatto woman to look for a man belonging to the privileged class and race. These two features of mulatto psychology, glimpsed by Villaverde over a hundred and fifty years ago, have been the subject of many subsequent works of literature.[20]

As far as the relationship between slave-owners and slaves is concerned, the picture presented is very much the same as in the other anti-slavery novels we have analysed. Villaverde emphasises not only the soulless cruelty of the slave-owners but their refusal to admit that Negroes are anything else than merchandise. Leonardo's father, for example, is seen speculating on the clandestine introduction of slaves into Cuba after the agreement of 1817 between England and Spain which gave the English the right to inspect Spanish merchant ships proceeding from Africa. Talking with his wife, Señor de Gamboa complains of the loss of some slaves who had to be thrown overboard because a warship was following the ship that was transporting them. The conversation in which Gamboa explains to his wife what has happened is calculated to horrify the reader. Even his wife is upset by such callous behaviour. 'Don't be foolish, woman,' he exclaims. 'Do you really expect me to believe that sacks of coal feel and suffer as we do? Nothing of the sort. How do you think they live over there in Africa? In caves and swamps.'[21]

But when he tells her that among the Negroes the sailors had thrown into the sea there was a twelve-year-old girl, the good lady is really upset and cries out: 'Oh, God's angels!' Her husband replies:

Do you really believe that those bundles from Africa have a soul and are angels? You are being blasphemous, Rosa. When the world realises that Negroes are animals and not men, the English will have no further justification for trying to stop the slave trade. It's the same in Spain with tobacco: they forbid its free entry into the country and those people who live off the tobacco smuggling, when they are hard pressed by the *carabineros*, throw away the tobacco and escape with their skins and their horses. Do you think tobacco has a soul? Do you think there is any difference between a sack of tobacco and a Negro, at least as far as feeling is concerned?[22]

From these passages it is clear that Villaverde not only intended to arouse indignation against the institution of slavery, but also to reveal the functioning of the mentality of the slave-owner. All the white characters in the book have a strong prejudice against Negroes, even Leonardo, who had taken Cecilia as a mistress without, of course, having the remotest intention of ever legalising his relationship with her. Cecilia, on the other hand, blinded in her pride at being a rich white man's mistress, had never realised this, thinking that by her beauty and her love she had conquered Leonardo.

The novel *Sab* (1841) by the well-known writer, Gertrudis Gómez de Avellaneda, resembles the novels of Suárez Romero, Zambrana and Villaverde in many important respects, except that the whole atmosphere of the book is profoundly romantic and sentimental in a way that the other novels are not. Her hero, Sab, is a man of noble sentiments, passionate and tender, ever ready to sacrifice himself for what he loves. At the same time he is something of a rebel, though his rebelliousness is largely verbal. Like so many romantic heroes he regards himself as cursed ('a terrible curse weighs on my existence because I am a mulatto and a slave'). He is of mysterious origins—a bastard and a slave, although his mother was born free and was a 'princess' in Africa. But although his body is that of a slave his soul is free and noble. He is impossibly in love with the white girl, Carlota. Sab is, in fact, a literary type rather than a Cuban slave painted direct from reality. The novel however contains a protest against slavery, which destroys the life of a generous and good man, and permits the survival and success of Sab's rival, a swindler and a char-latan. And it is precisely his condition as a slave that shuts Sab off from happiness, which he would have found in marrying Carlota. This is his 'curse' and there is no way out of it. Without his colour and his condition as a slave, Sab would have been a good and intelligent man, passionate and romantic by nature.

The author, besides her implicit protest against the evils of slavery, criticises the institution itself although differently from the other Cuban writers. While Suárez Romero, Zambrana and Villaverde all offer the reader scenes of repugnant cruelty and exhibit the wretched mentality of the slave-owners, Doña Gertrudis makes a theoretical and humanitarian criticism. Slavery is unjust, she feels, because it inspires pity in a sensitive and good soul. The following quotations will give the general tone of the work. 'Yes,' she exclaims, 'indeed, the sight of degraded humanity is a cruel spectacle. Men changed into beasts who bear on their brows the mark of slavery and in their souls the despair of Hell.' And her heroine, watching her own slaves who seem happy and contented (for apparently the atrocities of Suárez Romero's 'delights of country life' do not have a place on her family's plantation), exclaims:

Poor unfortunate things. They think they are lucky because they are not beaten and humiliated and they eat the bread of slavery in tranquillity. They think they are well off, and their children are slaves before they leave their mothers' wombs, and they can be sold like animals. When I am married no unfortunate man anywhere near me will breathe the poisoned air of slavery.[23]

Sab, the romantic Sab, at times gives free rein to his imagina-tion and has dreams of violence and revenge: 'The slaves drag their chains with patience: but to break them perhaps all they need is to hear a voice shouting: "You are men.",[24] And in an even more rebellious vein:

I have sometimes thought of setting against our oppressors the chained arms of their victims; of throwing among them the terrible cry of freedom and revenge. I have dreamed of bathing myself in the blood of the whites, of trampling under my feet their corpses and their laws and of dying myself among the ruins.[25]

This vision of violence and revenge, in which Sab sees him-self as leading a revolt and dying among the ruins, is a typically romantic piece of self-dramatisation, a flight of the imagination which leads to nothing concrete. For Sab is totally dominated by his exclusive passion for Carlota. These passages, nevertheless, can be taken as a warning on the part of the author, as she mentions directly what had happened a few years previously in Haiti, where the slaves in fact had revolted and massacred their white masters. She also makes it clear that the Haitian experience was a source of uneasiness and fear among the slave-owners in Cuba. Sab, then, is a romantic hero, suffering under the curse of his colour and his condition as a slave, and dreaming impotently of dramatic revenge, but there is very little of the Negro or mulatto in his psychology or way of being. This of course is precisely the argument of Doña Gertrudis: Sab is first and foremost a man in love. He is kind and generous but has had the misfortune of being born a slave and of bearing the stigma of a dark skin. Closer in spirit to the works of Suárez Romero, Villaverde and Zambrana is a curious book entitled *Coloured Poets*, by Francisco Calcagno, of which there were four editions, in 1868 in the periodical *La Revolución*, in 1878, 1879 and 1887. The profit on the 1879 edition was used to purchase the freedom of the slave poet, José de Carmen Díaz. The book is made up of biographical notes on four coloured poets who were all born slaves. Of these, the best known was Gabriel de la Concepción Valdés ('Plácido') who was executed as a conspirator by the Spanish Government; the other three were Agustín Baldomero Rodríguez, Juan Francisco Manzano and Antonio Medina. The most interesting part of this collection is the autobiography of the poet, Juan Francisco Manzano, who tells in his own words of the first thirty years of his life.

This account of the sufferings of an intelligent and fairly well educated slave is one of the most valuable documents of the period, written as it is from the inside as a protest against the injustices of slavery. Certain features of the life of a slave stand out very sharply, such as the constant insecurity, the absolute dependence on the whims of the masters, the arbitrariness of the masters and the slave's difficulty in obtaining justice when accused of a crime. For example, Manzano tells of how he was accused of the theft of a chicken. He denies his guilt but is tortured and punished in an effort to force him to admit how and when he had committed the theft. Later it is discovered that he is innocent but before this he has been submitted to extremely brutal treatment and has no opportunity of appeal. The deepest impressions left by this autobiographical sketch are of the arbitrariness and meanness of the masters, and the total denial of any kind of rights to the slave.

Manzano's story had a curious history as it was first published in 1840 in an English translation, in the same volume as several of his poems also translated into English. The author of the English translation was Dr. Richard Madden, already referred to in this chapter. The book also contained poems by Madden himself, which deal with the horrors of slavery, very much in the tone of Suárez Romero's *Francisco*—scenes of the brutal treatment of slaves on the plantations and a picture of the cynical and callous attitude of the slave-owners.

From this analysis of the nineteenth-century Cuban anti-slavery novel, it is possible to see an ideological current of protest against the institution of slavery. It is depicted, on the moral plane, as inhuman, contrary to the laws of nature, and as demoralising not only the slaves but also the masters. Political calculation was not, of course, lacking, as the Cuban liberals hoped to enlist the support of the black masses in their fight against Spanish domination. This was shown by the freeing of slaves by the Cuban rebels in 1868, and it appeared to be justified by the struggles against Spain in 1898 in which the black masses played an important part in the final defeat of the Spaniard. Thus slavery, like Indianism, was used as a weapon against Spanish domination. Nevertheless, the majority of the unpleasant characters who are shown as the immediate instruments of the sufferings of the slaves are not Spaniards but Cubans. This point is made explicitly by Zambrana in his *Francisco*:

> Let them concern themselves less with Spanish domination, and pay more attention to the condition of the Negro. Let them worry less about being exploited, and more about exploiting. The slavery one suffers is a terrible thing, but an even more terrible thing is the slavery one is imposing. You say: 'Ah, if only Cubans were not slaves.' I say, 'If only they did not own slaves.'[26]

The writers of the anti-slavery novels were all white Cubans, if we exclude Manzano's autobiographical account of his life as a slave, and we may ask ourselves, how did these non-coloured writers see the Negro, bearing in mind that they were all looking at the Negro from the outside, that is to say, that they did not live with the Negroes, nor lead the same kind of life, and most probably had very little intimate contact with them?

Sab, as we have seen, is a romantic type cursed by his condition as a slave and by the colour of his skin, but apart from that he is an Hernani, a Don Alvaro, a Lorenzaccio of the romantic school, as are most of the characters in Avellaneda's novels. Suárez Romero's Francisco, more than anything else, is the victim of a system; all his misfortunes are in fact attributable to the existence of slavery. All he wants to do is to lead a normal life. His final suicide, when he learns of Dorotea's sacrifice, has a romantic flavour about it. Villaverde's slaves are also victims of a system, with little character or personality of their own. On the other hand, his analysis of the psychology of the free mulattos is much in advance of anything to be found in Suárez Romero or Avellaneda. But it is only in Zambrana's *Francisco* that a serious attempt is made to give the Negro a distinctive personality. Francisco is rough and primitive, conscious of being a Negro, and proud of his race. Both he, with his magnificent physique ('an ebony Apollo'), and Camila with her fiery and overwhelming sensuality, are characters possessing a clearly defined racial personality.

The culmination of almost a century of writing on the colour question in Cuba is to be found in the works of José Martí. As the ideological founder of free Cuba, Martí was naturally concerned with the racial problem in Cuba. As a liberal politician, he was in favour of the freeing of the slaves, whom he wanted as friends of the Cuban independence movement, but he also realised that after independence white and coloured Cubans would have to go on living together, and as the far-seeing maker of a Cuban national ideology, he wanted all Cubans, whatever their race, to live together in peace and harmony. He saw the sacrifices of the war of independence as unifying all Cubans into one indivisible people: 'In war, in face of death, all barefooted and all naked, Negroes and whites became equal. After this embrace, they have not become separate again.'[27] As might have been expected, the theme of slavery in Martí ran along anti-Spanish lines:

> The sublime emancipation of the slaves by their Cuban masters wiped out, through brotherhood in death of masters and slaves, all the hatred engendered by slavery.[28]

Spain was deaf, and the only nation in the world which continued to maintain slavery. The terrible truth was there. The black man in Cuba was a slave. The whip rose with the sun every day. Men were herded like animals, punished, made to breed, torn to pieces by dogs on the roads. This is how the black man lived in Cuba before the revolution.[29]

But Martí, poet and philosopher as he was, looked into the future of Cuba and further still into the future of humanity. In another article, 'My Race', published in the magazine *Patria* in New York in 1893, he wrote on the racial question with a profound and far-seeing universal vision:

The white racialist who believes he has superior rights, what justification has he for complaining of the black racialist? The black racialist who thinks his race is specially endowed, what right has he to complain of the white racialist? The white man who by reason of his race believes himself superior to the black man admits the idea of race, and justifies and provokes the black racialist. The black man who proclaims his race, when what he really means to proclaim, although using this erroneous expression, is the spiritual identity of all races, justifies and provokes the white racialist. Peace demands the common rights of nature for all: differential rights, contrary to nature, are the enemies of peace. The white man who isolates himself also isolates the black man. The black man who isolates himself isolates and provokes the white man. In Cuba there is no danger of a race war. Man is more than white, more than mulatto, more than black. Cuban is more than white, more than mulatto, more than black. . . . True men, white or black, will treat each other with loyalty and kindness because they appreciate virtue and because they take a pride in everything that honours the land in which we were born.[30]

Slavery virtually ended in Cuba in 1869 when the revolutionaries declared it abolished and freed their slaves; and legally in 1886, when it was abolished by the Spanish Government. The struggle, which had lasted for nearly a century, took the form not only of novels and articles, but of almost constant guerrilla warfare. But once slavery was abolished, men of high humanitarian ideals like Martí went beyond the Cuban situation and proclaimed the unity of the human race. Martí's thought shaped to a large extent the Cuban independence movement, and in his voluminous writings, mostly published in newspapers and periodicals, he gave Cuba a sort of national ideology, which has informed liberal thought there ever since. Even during the Castro revolution quotations from Martí were as much in evidence as slogans launched by Castro himself. It is indeed no exaggeration to say that Martí's works have served and continue to serve as a political and ideological Bible in Cuba. And his attitude to the colour question, both in Cuba and in general, can be seen as a fitting culmination to almost a century of writing which condemned the inhumanity of slavery and which created an atmosphere in which the fine flower of Martí's thought could flourish.

Slavery had ended in Haiti in 1804, in the British Caribbean territories by 1834 and in Cuba, its last stronghold, in 1886, and after this anti-slavery literature lost its *raison d'être*. Nevertheless, slavery as a subject of literature continued between 1900 and 1960. As a subject or an allusion it appears particularly in poems of protest against the cruelty and the hypocrisy of the white world in general, and in poems inspired in the spirit of anti-colonialism and anti-imperialism. This does not apply only to the British and French territories, which remained colonies until the mid-twentieth century, but also to Cuba, where, though independent since 1898, there is deep-rooted anti-imperialist feeling against the United States—a feeling finally given political expression in Fidel Castro's revolution, which presents itself as a movement of independence from American colonial domination. The preoccupation with Africa as a lost fatherland also often involves allusions to the slave-trade and slavery. This is particularly true of Haiti, where emotional Africanism is strong.

In his poem 'Me revoici, Harlem', the Haitian poet Jean Brierre speaks to the Negroes of the United States, recalling their common sufferings in the past:

> Together we knew the horror of the slave-ships,
> and often like me you feel cramps
> awaking after the murderous centuries
> and you feel the old wounds bleed in your flesh.[31]

Another Haitian, Roussan Camille, in 'Les soutiers noirs', on a ship in Dakar, hearing the singing of the Negro bunker-hands, is reminded of the journey of his own African ancestors from Africa:

> The ship was singing so loudly
> in the effervescence of cocktails
> and the careless gaiety of laughter,

the sea was so choppy
as it slapped against the hull,
the orders were so rapid—

.  .  .  .  .

—your tortured songs
the same we sang on another voyage
from distant Africa
to the Atlantic isles
where—their arms tied—
were fatigue and suffering.[32]

In panoramic poems covering the whole of the Caribbean (a common enough subject in Caribbean writing) the memory of the days of slavery almost inevitably appears, as in the poem, 'The Indies', by the Barbadian, Slade Hopkinson:

Then the men they brought
African kings trading their subjects.
And Europe scattered round the saucer of the sea,
dust, cane, blood, leather; and the sun
shedding sneers like a cynic.
Khaki more powerful than purple, the black
silhouette of the man pinned on the sky-line
bearing the sun's weight on his back like a cross;
and at night
the blanket of grief, and the turn to sleep,
for relief.[33]

The well-known poem 'Elegía' by Nicolás Guillén evokes slavery in a series of bitter, vivid images:

Over the sea
came the pirate
messenger of the devil,
with his steady, fixed stare
and his monotonous wooden leg.
Over the sea came the pirate.

We must learn to remember
what the clouds cannot forget.

Over the sea
with the hyacinth and the bull,
with flour and iron

came the Negro, to make gold;
and to weep in his exile.
Over the sea came the pirate.

How can you forget
what the clouds can still remember?

Over the sea
the parchments of the law,
the rod for fraudulent measuring,
and the whip to punish,
and the pox of the viceroy,
and death, to sleep
without waking,
Over the sea.

A hard thing to remember
what the clouds cannot forget
over the sea.[34]

The Cuban José Rodríguez Méndez in his *Poemas del Batey*
gives the usual description of the sufferings and humiliation of
the slaves, but claims that the slavery of the Negro in Cuba did
not end but continued under another form:

The lash of the overseer punished our sides with fear
so we would walk with the docility of bridled ponies
along with the oxen
we also died like animals
punished by the goad of the slaver.
And to 'console' us for our ulcerated sores
they used to talk about Heaven.

Today we are still slaves
because we sweat and tear our hands
for a cheap wage.[35]

In the *Poésies nationales* (Paris, 1892) by the Haitian, Massill-
lon Coicou, there are various poems inspired by slavery. In 'Le
supplice des noirs', he describes with abundance of detail the
public torturing and death of the Haitian revolutionaries,
Chavannes and Ogé, who were publicly broken on the wheel.
Coicou paints his scene deliberately stressing the sadistic cruelty
of the French colonialists. His thesis is that the cruelty of the

French explains and justifies the excesses and atrocities of the Haitian revolutionaries:

> Do not dare reproach the Negro for his excesses,
> Do not dare to curse him, and understand his hatred.[36]

So we see the theme of slavery outliving abolition all over the Caribbean and becoming almost a cliché. It is likely that as a subject it will die hard, particularly considering that the present orientation of much Caribbean writing is anti-European and in many cases anti-white. It also fits in well with the denunciations of colonialism and imperialism which are increasingly common in Cuba and the French West Indian islands.

# CHAPTER II

# AFRO-CUBANISM

As we saw in the last chapter, the Negro was an important figure in the anti-slavery literature of Cuba. It was natural enough that writers should have been concerned with the Negro slave, as he was in the foreground of a set of social and political conditions which the *avant-garde* of the Cuban intellectuals were seeking to change. However, in the period 1920–40, the Negro, with his social and cultural background, not only figures prominently on the Cuban literary scene, but indeed tends to dominate it. For the Negro to have become the main subject of literature and painting in Haiti, Jamaica or Martinique would have been natural and logical, as the majority of the people in these countries are of predominantly African descent. But in Cuba the Negroes are a minority, so the explanation of Afro-Cubanism clearly cannot be sought in the ethnic or social conditions of Cuba. Interest in the Negro in Cuban literature of this period in fact is largely a literary phenomenon, at least within the bounds of the Afro-Cuban movement, although, particularly in the later phase of its development, the Negro appears in a social context, and a strong note of protest against racial discrimination is heard above the sound of the drums and the *maracas*.

The cult of the primitive, endemic in European culture since the Renaissance, took possession of the arts in Europe to an unprecedented degree in the decade following the First World War. As early as 1910, Leo Frobenius had published his *Black Decameron*, and Picasso and the Cubists had undergone the influence of African sculpture. Other works by Frobenius continued to call attention to the value of African art. Indeed, in the years following the First World War, we are confronted with a critical reaction against the whole of Western culture, in literature, painting, historiography and psychology. Surrealism had attempted to break the strength of the Graeco-Latin and Christian tradition in the arts, and welcomed with enthusiasm the deformities of Yoruba or Congo sculpture. The theories of Sigmund

Freud himself strengthened the anti-intellectualist current since they gave the impression that the unhappiness, neurosis and frustration of the peoples of the West were the outcome of the excessive repression of the primordial instincts. No doubt the disillusionment caused by the war contributed to the discredit of European culture, as it appeared to many people that so many centuries of science, philosophy and humanitarian theorising had culminated in the most atrocious war humanity had ever known. The German philosopher-historian Oswald Spengler's *Decline of the West* must be mentioned here, as his theories on the failure of Western civilisation had direct repercussions on the thought of some Caribbean writers involved in the Afro-Cuban movement. The literary fashion for the primitive was bound up with this complex of ideas and theories, and in the arts the African found a preferential place, but also, to a lesser degree, the Negro of the United States and of Latin America.[1]

But although, as is recognised by many Afro-Cuban writers, the initial impulse for the Cuban cult of the primitive is a derivative of the European fashion, the movement had a very important precursor in Fernando Ortiz. Already in 1906 with his *Negro Sorcerers* and in 1916 with his *The Negro Slaves*, Ortiz had probed deeply into the life of the Negro element in Cuban society, and although his methods were completely academic, his discussion of the customs, religious beliefs, dances, songs, musical instruments and psychology of the Cuban Negro made fascinating and exotic reading for both Cuban and foreigner. In 1924 he published his *Glosario de afronegrismos*, a collection of African or African-sounding words in the popular speech of Cuba and of words of Spanish origin with new Cuban meanings. Many of these words have a markedly African rhythmic sonority (*cumbancha, simbombo, chévere, sandunga, mondongo*, etc.) and are to be found some years later in the compositions of the Afro-Cuban writers. It seems certain that these works of Ortiz helped attract the attention of Cuban intellectuals to the rich vein of Negro folklore in Cuba and to open new perspectives on the artistic and literary potentialities of Cuban popular art in general. And it was precisely the atmosphere of Afro-Cuban dancing, singing and superstition that appeared as the main constituents in literature when, to use a phrase of Ortiz: 'In 1928 the drums begin to beat in Cuban poetry.'[2]

Although Ortiz can be seen as a precursor of Afro-Cubanism, and his influence throughout the movement is undeniable, the main influence was definitely the European fashion for the primitive and for Negro art. This is recognised by many Cuban writers, but they make a distinction. When they took up the European fashion for Negro art, they claim, they did so with more sincerity than Europeans, for Negro art had a deeper significance for them. The Cuban Negro is Cuban and his art and mode of being, his special sensibility, are part of the basic patrimony of the people of Cuba. Some also saw in Afro-Cubanism a road to a deeper level of Cubanism and a means of making a characteristically Cuban contribution to universal culture. In an essay, 'On an Important Cuban Matter', Juan Marinello writes:

> The search for the autochthonous and its expression, indigenism, which we observe in a great deal of contemporary Hispanoamerican art, have no roots in Cuba, because there is no Indian population and our extinct Indians have left no architecture or literature. The Negro, a universal theme and motive, on the other hand, has in Cuba a specific significance. His participation in Cuban life was decisive in the revolution against Spain; his social tragedy, a new slavery, makes him the object of meditation and hope. His physical characteristics, enriched and multiplied in his mixing with the white and the yellow man, his dances of a subtle and enchanting primitivism, make him the object of the greatest artistic potentialities.[3]

And the same Marinello in *Poetics, Essays in Enthusiasm* writes:

> Cuban poets, contemporary Cuban poets, have a great responsibility: to give to the continent the song of the Negro with its present anguish and in the bright anticipation of its destiny. No country as much as ours possesses the possibility of this work of art and humanity. Here the Negro is marrow and root, the breath of the people, a music heard, and irrepressible impulse. He may, in these times of change, be the touchstone of our poetry.[4]

In the prologue to his anthology of Afro-Cuban poetry Ramón Guirao affirms the special significance of Negro art for Cuba at the same time as he admits its European origin:

> The Negro fashion was not born in Cuba, as in Europe, without a tradition and removed from the human document. Bilingual poetry of Spanish and African dialects has a historical dimension and an undefined future, and linked with Creole sensibility, it may form the great vernacular poetry of which we were speaking.[5]

The Afro-Cubanists welcomed the primitivism of the Negro as a positive quality and some pronounced themselves in favour of Negro primitivism as a corrective to the over-civilisation of the white world with its unhappiness, frustrations and inhibitions, taking up a position in the anti-intellectual current to which we have referred. In an article entitled 'More about Mulatto Poetry' Fernando Ortiz eulogises the rumba in the following terms, which leave no doubt about his attitude. As far as he is concerned, the rumba is a liberation, a release through therapeutic action, and he speaks poetically, if vaguely, of a 'transparent metaphysic':

The rumba is the release of over-abundant force of life in a frenzy of all the muscles: it is the hypnosis of music which embraces with the magic of its rhythms. The rumba is an unleashing of human tensions only restrained in its supreme harmony. The human bow bent to shoot the arrows of life to all horizons, to its maximum tension, and any further tension would cause it to snap.[6]

In an Afro-Cuban novel, *Ecué-Yamba-O*, Alejo Carpentier traces the life of a Negro boy who lives entirely in the enchanted world of *santería*, or Cuban voodoo. Far from feeling humble and inferior, he derives a sense of superiority from this fact. As he puts it: 'Among the Americans, *Sarambambiche* ('son-of-a-bitch', the Hispanicised version of the expression typifies Americans to him), he felt real pride in his primitive life, full of complications and magic subtleties which the men of the North never understood.'[7] This theoretical enthronement of the primitivism of the Negro runs parallel with the production of poems, stories, and novels in which sensuality and emotionalism predominate. The very first manifestation of the movement is to be found in the Puerto Rican writer Luis Palés Matos, who in March 1926 published his 'Negro Town' in *Los Sábados de la Democracia* of San Juan. This poem contains almost all the features of subsequent Afro-Cuban writing: dynamic sensuality, a realistic carnality and a purely rhythmical use of language. In an article 'The Art of the White Race' he echoes the theories of Spengler:

The aesthetic sense of the white race has reached a stage of dangerous cerebralisation....I do not believe in a monumental art of purely cerebral representation: I only believe in an art which identifies itself with the thing and fuses with the essence of the thing. An art which is as little art as possible, that is, where the aptitude for creation is subjected to the urge of the blood and instinct, which is always the right urge, because it carries with it the tho sands of years of experience of the species.[8]

And he goes on to speak of the decadence of Western art in terms that are completely Spenglerian. In another article, 'Towards a Caribbean Poetry', he returns to the subject of primitive art, pointing out its rightness, its suitability in the Caribbean:

> In any corner of the planet where there are men, that is a rhythm of life, an interplay of passions, a ferment of interest in movement, a work of art can appear. The important thing is that the creative genius of the artist should tear from the environment that surrounds him his main accents which reach the very essence of humanity.[9]

Now, Palés Matos ascribes to the Negro a vital role in the formation of Caribbean culture, the Negro who, as he puts it, 'lives physically and spiritually within us all', and he attributes to him the function of a precipitating agent, adding that 'his characteristics, filtered through the mulatto, influence in a very apparent manner every manifestation of the life of our people'.[10]

From the very beginning (Palés Matos's 'Negro Dance', 1926, and José Z. Tallet's 'Rumba', 1928) the principal features of Afro-Cuban poetry had been established, and there is little variation or development in its basic constituents; at most there are differences of emphasis. In such poets as José Z. Tallet, Emilio Ballagas, Nicolás Guillén, Alejo Carpentier, Ramón Guirao, we find Negro figures, male and female, caught in the frantic contortions of Afro-Cuban dancing. There are music, drums, *maracas*, *güiros*, guitars, rum-drinking, voodoo possession and sometimes crimes of violence; the maddening rhythms of the drums shake the dancers in an atmosphere of rum and sweat as they writhe in distorted arabesques. Some of the poets, through the use of words of purely rhythmic value, attempt to reproduce the hypnotic physical effect of the movement of the dance. The setting is the lowest stratum of Cuban social life, either urban or rural, the level at which the majority of Cuban Negroes lived in the 1920s and 1930s. There is a noticeable insistence on the animality of the dancers' movements of hips, contortions of muscles, in an atmosphere charged with sexuality, alcohol and sometimes voodoo. The typical female rumba dancer, as in Tallet's well-known 'Rumba', is described in purely physical terms: 'She moves one buttock and then the other', she 'shoots out her rump' (the Spanish word *grupa* is normally used of an animal). He refers to the 'powerful haunches' (*ancas,* usually of horses), of the appearance of her movements. The following two quotations are very typical of the crude physicality and indeed the whole atmosphere of the Afro-Cuban dance as described by the poets:

> And the niña Tomasa writhes
> and there is a smell of jungle
> and there is a smell of Negro sweat
> and there is a smell of males
> and there is a smell of females
> and there is a smell of city tenements
> and there is a smell of country barrack-houses.
> And the two heads are two dry coco-nuts
> on which somebody has written with lime
> above, a diaeresis, below a dash.
> And the two bodies of the two Negroes
> are two mirrors of sweat.[11]

The following quotation from a poem by Alfonso Hernández Catá could almost serve as a parody of the Afro-Cuban manner:

> However much dressed she is
> the black statue is visible,
> eyes of sea-shell
> and lips of raw steak.
>
> Her waist grinds desires
> and strange words escape from her lips,
> a hundred eyes seek the roads
> which lead to her inside.
>
> Africa weeps in the orchestra,
> a humid torpor presses down.
> Under the whip-lash of the tropics,
> Aryan pride bows down.[12]

In Palés Matos there is the same insistence on sexual animality and in 'Negro Village' he even gives his Negroes an African background with elephants, hippopotami and baobab trees:

> Mussumba, Timbuctu, Farafangana,
> unreal village of peace and sleep.
>
> Someone dissolves lazily
> into the wind a monorhythmic song.

.        .        .        .        .

It is the Negro woman who is singing
her sober life as a domestic animal:
the black woman of the regions of the sun,
who smells of earth, game and sex.
It is the Negro woman who is singing
and her sensual song spreads around
like a clear atmosphere of happiness
under the shade of the coconut trees.[13]

And as if to leave no room for doubt as to the primitiveness of
the Negro, in a poem called 'Ñam-Ñam' he boldly proclaims
the unintellectual, animal nature of the Negro:

Asia dreams its nirvana
America dances its jazz,
Europe plays and theorises,
Africa grunts: ñam-ñam.[14]

In all these poems the Negro appears reduced to an animal,
instinctive level. Indeed the overwhelming impression left by the
writers of the Afro-Cuban movement is that the Negro was little
more than a doll or a puppet which they made to jump and writhe
about to the accompaniment of Cuban popular instruments.
It is not surprising to find a coloured poet, the Chinese mulatto
Regino Pedroso, raising his voice in angry protest against this
exclusive use of the Negro as a dancing figure. In his 'Brother
Negro' he is clearly protesting against this aspect of Afro-
Cubanism:

For their pleasure
the rich man makes a toy of you.
And in Paris, in New York, and in Madrid and Havana
like bibelots,
they make straw Negroes for export.

And he asks:

Are we nothing more than Negro?
Are we nothing more than music and noise?
Are we only rumba, black lust and carnival bands?
Are we nothing more than grimaces and colour?
Grimaces and colour?

And the poem ends:

> Give to the world your cry of rebellion,
> your human voice—
> and stop playing your maracas so much.[15]

The case of Nicolás Guillén deserves special attention. Guillén belonged to the Afro-Cuban movement, was a contemporary of Tallet, Ballagas, Guirao, etc., and wrote in the same reviews, and up to a point he shares with them the same technical devices: use of words for rhythmical effect, atmosphere of the dance and of course the Negro theme. But of all the Afro-Cuban writers, Nicolás Guillén was a coloured man, a mulatto, and as Cintio Vitier points out, the great difference is that he writes 'from within', and the Negro theme is not just a fashion, a subject for literature, but the living heart of his creative activity.[16] Even so, in many of his early poems, we find the characteristic atmosphere of dancing and sex, an external, plastic vision of the Negro. But in and after *West Indies Ltd.* (1934) his poetry is infused with a growing concern for the social and economic position of the Negro in Cuba, and while he does not abandon the popular tone and the general manner of Afro-Cuban poetry, he 'wipes the alcohol off the guitar's mouth' and tells it to play 'its full song'. And he tells Sabas, 'the harmless Negro', the big, easy-going Sabas, not to be so easy-going or so simple, and to stop begging:

> Take your bread, do not beg for it.
> Take your light, take your definite hope
> like a horse by the bridle.[17]

In poems like 'The Song of the Bongo' and the 'Ballad of my Two Grandfathers', he affirms the oneness of the Cuban people through miscegenation and in 'The Two Children' the unity of black and white through poverty and exploitation.

> Two children, branches of the same tree of poverty,
> eating in a door-way under the torrid night.[18]

In Guillén, then, we find both the Afro-Cuban world of dancing, drumming, alcoholic frenzy, elements of Cuban folklore ('The Ballad of the Güije' and 'Sensemayá') and poems of social and racial protest. The second phase is seen by Guillén himself as a maturing of his early manner, but still, as already pointed out, a lot of the Afro-Cuban mannerisms are retained, particularly rhythmic repetitions in the style of Cuban popular songs (the rumba, *son*, *guaracha*) and racy Cuban turns of speech. For Guillén wanted to reach the Cuban people through his poetry, and he felt that these elements were a ready means of communication. Although the protest against colour discrimination is constant, Guillén never adopted aggressive anti-white attitudes. His message is 'Accept us for what we are'. Thus, in one of his most moving poems, 'My Country is Sweet on the Outside' from *El son entero*, he offers his hand in friendship to Chinese, black and white. But when an American sailor in a bar wants to hit him, with simple dramatism he kills the American:

> He wanted to hit me with his hand
> He wanted to hit me with his hand
> But there he remained, dead,
> Good but there he remained dead.[19]

It was not only in the work of Guillén that Afro-Cubanism evolved into a militant literature of protest against discrimination. In 1937 was founded the *Revista de Estudios Afro-Cubanos* which published four numbers between 1937 and 1940. The aim of this review was to study the contribution of the Negro to Cuban life and to analyse the phenomena produced in the island as a result of contact between the two ethnic groups. In an article 'Religion in Mulatto Poetry' (vol. I, 1937), Fernando Ortiz deals with racial prejudice as it exists in Cuba and in another article (vol. III, 1938) Ortiz also insists on the essential Cuban-ness of the Negro, affirming his importance to Cuba as an integral part of Cuban life. Other articles in the review deal with such questions as Afro-Cuban religious beliefs and practices, and dancing and music. There are also Cuban Negro folk-tales by Lydia Cabrera and an article on 'Racial Prejudice in Puerto Rico' (vol. II, 1938) by the Puerto Rican Tomás Blanco. In 1947, Fernando Ortiz published his *Deception of Racialism*, an analysis and criticism of racial concepts and a denunciation of Fascist racialism. There is very little new or original in this book, but it is a powerful attack on racial prejudice, supported by Ortiz's vast erudition. In 1943, J. A. Fernández de Castro published his *The Negro Theme in Cuban Literature*, in which, apart from discussing the subject, he insists that it is still very much alive: 'The hour of the Negro in literature is not over, as some snobs claim, as if it were a mere literary fashion.'[20] Nevertheless, the Afro-Cuban movement with the characteristic features we have described, can be said to have been ended by 1940. Writing in *Revista Cubana* in 1946, Emilio Ballagas said: 'The Afro-Cuban movement can be considered as liquidated, after about ten years of existence, in 1940. It did not perish, but was incorporated into Cuban poetry, possibly to form a more substantial movement.'[21]

And indeed, Afro-Cubanism seems to be completely worked out by 1940. It produced its best work in the period 1926–38, but looking at the movement in the perspective of history, the crop of works of lasting literary value is disappointingly small. The best of it, that is the artistically most successful part of Afro-Cubanism, is to be found in the works of Nicolás Guillén and Luis Palés Matos. Apart from this, we are left with a handful of poems by Tallet, Guirao, Carpentier and Ballagas. A great deal of the products of Afro-Cubanism have, in fact, the air of a literary fad, and are very repetitious in matter and style.

The movement was born, as we have seen, from the conjunction of the fashion for the primitive of the 1920s and from a characteristically Latin American desire for literary novelty and originality. The Negro was to have played the part played by the Indian, the *indígena* in the literature of such countries as Mexico, Ecuador and Peru, opening up the way towards a deeper expression of the Cuban soul and making possible a fuller integration of the Cuban national personality, and undoubtedly the most valuable contribution of Afro-Cubanism was a realisation in Cuba of the role of the Negro in the over-all life of the Cuban people, and particularly in popular art. Again it was Guillén and Ortiz who seem to have understood this situation most fully. In an essay 'Mulatto Poetry', Ortiz sees the social and artistic problem of the Negro in Cuba as 'a process of understanding ourselves, of delving into ourselves, of national integration'.[22] Ortiz was also fully aware of the racial prejudice existing in Cuba and was quite explicit about it, while many Cubans refused to admit it existed; at the same time he emphasised the value of the Negro's contribution in popular music and dancing, and also in all sorts of habits, customs and attitudes—to the character and personality of the Cuban people. Guillén's work in many respects appears as an artistic transposition of the ideas of Ortiz—a utilisation and adaptation of popular and folk-lore elements, an evaluation of the Negro's part in Cuban life. Like Ortiz he claims recognition for the Cuban Negro as an integral part of Cuban life. The beating of the bongo calls to black and white alike, as part of the Cuban historical experience, and his black grandfather, Taita Facundo, and his white grand-father, Don Federico, are pictured as united by the same funda-mental human anguish:

> Shadows that only I can see
> my two grandfathers go with me.
>
> Don Federico shouts to me
> and Taita Facundo is silent;
> and both dream on through the night,
> I bring them together.
> Federico
> Facundo. They both embrace.
> They both sigh. They both
> raise their proud heads
> under the high stars;
> both of the same stature.
> Black anguish and white anguish
> both of the same stature.
> And they shout. And dream. And weep. And sing.
> And sing – and sing – and sing.[23]

The Afro-Cuban or Afro-Antillian movement did not pass entirely without criticism. In 1932, in Puerto Rico, at the height of the enthusiasm for Negro art, J. I. de Diego Padró wrote in *El Mundo* of San Juan a slashing attack on the Negro fashion, describing it as due to a 'lack of mental balance' and 'a morbid attempt to be original'.[24]

The Dominican poet, Manuel del Cabral, in the prologue to his *On this Side of the Sea* denounces the Negro fashion in abusive terms. Answering his own question: 'What about the coloured man in our continent?' he answers: 'There is a Negro raggle-taggle going round these countries, a rhetoric of colour rest-ing on the physical basis of the word. . . . Is there an American art? Is there a Negro poetry? I feel I must deny the existence of both.'[25] Nevertheless, Cabral himself had published a volume of poems with the title of *Twelve Negro Poems,* in which images similar to those used by the Afro-Cubans are not lacking. The rumba dancer in his 'Barbarous Music' cannot be differentiated from the sensual dancing dolls of Tallet, Guirao, etc.

> Go on, black girl, go on,
> with the earth-quake of your belly.
> Flesh of cane brandy, bongo body.
> The jungle bursts out, from your waist,
> to the paradise of your biting teeth.[26]

Cabral seems fascinated by the Negro theme and returns to it repeatedly, although generally to emphasise the primitive aspects of the Negro in a negative sense—his simplicity, his submissiveness. To Cabral, the Negro is a child, an elemental force ('neither the child nor the ass has your simplicity'), and he laughs at the Haitian witch-doctor with his paraphernalia of charms and incantations, but who nevertheless is a poor beggar:

> Haitian witch-doctor
> you work miracles with your black candle
> you say,
> I hold the future in my hands,
> Yes—
> Haitian witch-doctor, the future,
> prisoner in the flame of your candle.
> But.
> And your poor man's smile?[27]

This is perhaps not surprising as the Dominican Republic was officially hostile to Afro-Antillianism in any form and, in a sort of compendium of information about the Dominican Republic put out by the Government, any idea of African influence in Dominican culture is roundly rejected. The following quotation leaves no room for doubt: 'It is not untrue to speak of Afro-Cuban, Afro-Brazilian, Afro-Haitian, or even Afro-North American culture; but it would never occur to anybody to speak of Afro-Dominican culture.'[28] According to this work, the Negro in the Dominican Republic (a very high percentage of the population) has been absorbed completely, has given up any African atavism and has adjusted to the system of Dominican culture which has deep Spanish roots. The racial type which gives its specific character to the Dominican people, the common denominator between the white Dominican and the Dominican of African ancestry, is the aboriginal Indian. It must be remembered that from 1930 to 1961, that is during the dictatorship of General Rafael Leonidas Trujillo, an official attitude in the Dominican Republic in such fields as history, literature, sociology, economics, held the force of law. Any infringement could bring severe punishment. Also fear of Haitian encroachments had led the Dominican Government to minimise any African connexions and to make every effort to 'hispanicise the rural masses'. Clearly, in such an atmosphere a movement like Afro-Cubanism could not flourish.

The anti-intellectual and primitivist revaluation of the Negro is a thing of the past, a closed chapter in Cuban literary history. It died because it could not renew itself thematically or in technique and the world of dancing and verbal drumming was soon exhausted. In its final phase it moved in the direction of a literature of protest, in the last analysis, against economic exploitation and discrimination in Cuba.

It is perhaps noteworthy that Afro-Cubanism of the kind we have been examining scarcely rippled the surface of the literatures of the British and French Caribbean and Haiti, although of course writing on the Negro theme was not lacking. It would appear that in these islands, where the majority of the population is Negro, the subject was not regarded as a literary fashion, a 'Negro moment', but as a deep-rooted concern bound up with every-day living and feeling: writers such as the Jamaican Claude McKay, the Haitian Jacques Roumain or the Martinican Aimé Césaire were generational contemporaries of Ballagas, Palés Matos, etc., and each in his own way was influenced by the Negro fashion in Europe and the United States. But they assimilated this influence in a very different way. They were attracted by the aesthetic and cultural aspects of Negro primitivism, but they saw it as a creative, regenerative agent, not as a momentary release of nervous tensions. They were led to seek a rehabilitation of Negro culture, both in Africa and in the New World, not as a novelty but as a basis for a constructive projection towards the future.

# CHAPTER III

# REJECTION OF EUROPEAN CULTURE AS A THEME IN CARIBBEAN LITERATURE

THE literature of the Caribbean islands, whether in Spanish, French or English, possesses a community of themes and of subject-matter which is no doubt due to similarities in historical and social development, and to similar ethnic composition. There is, for instance, the theme of the slaves' journey from Africa, with its inevitable attendant horrors; the master and slave relationship; the theme of nostalgia for the imaginary lost fatherland, Africa; there is the anti-imperialist theme which invariably takes the form of the oppression and persecution of an individual, family or small community by the representative of a powerful foreign company. Usually the small man goes down, though he may go down fighting. The object of this kind of writing is to produce indignation. The treatment of 'nature', the sensuous, pleasant Caribbean tropics, is a commonplace of all the literatures of the area. With slight variations of emphasis, these themes appear in the writing of all the Caribbean islands.

The theme it is the object of this chapter to deal with is what I have called the rejection of European culture. It has been handled by a sufficiently great number of the more outstanding writers of the area to make it worthy of analysis. Whether it is a theme which will continue to be treated in varying ways, or whether it will later be seen as a response to a passing phase in the growth of a Caribbean consciousness would at present be difficult to predict. The objection that the idea of jettisoning European culture in favour of African values (which are suggested as a replacement) is absurd and impracticable is beside the point. In any case, we are not concerned with whether writers are right or wrong, but with analysing how the theme is presented, with what its possible cultural origins are, and with trying to define its temporal limits. That there is a powerful emotional and possibly political drive behind this theme is obvious, and need not be discussed here.

To start with, let us see how this theme appears in the writers of various countries. In Haiti, Cuba and the Dominican Republic, which had already developed a fairly abundant literature in the course of the nineteenth century, we find in the writings of Salomé Ureña de Henriquez, Cirilo Villaverde, Galván and Suárez Romero repeated attacks on the European colonial powers for the cruelty with which they first killed the Indians and then brought Negro slaves from Africa, subjecting them subsequently to all the horrors of slave labour. These attacks cannot, however, be interpreted as a rejection of European values. They are fundamentally political writings, which aim at forming a national consciousness. The Cuban and the Dominican clearly identifies himself with the Indians who were hounded by the Spaniards and who tried to defend their lives and lands against the foreign usurper. Haiti, which had enjoyed a precarious independence since 1804, naturally felt the need to form a national consciousness in the face of possible imperialist aggression. But this is not the same thing as a rejection of European cultural values in favour of African ones.

One of the very first voices raised in praise of Africa was that of the Haitian, Anténor Firmin, who in his *De l'égalité des races humaines* points to the great achievements of the ancient Egyptians who, he claims, were black people of Ethiopian origin. Efforts on the part of European anthropologists to prove that the ancient Egyptians were not black are due, according to Firmin, to racial prejudice: '... every imaginable subtlety has been brought to play, every quibble has been built up into sound argument, every possible erudite subterfuge has been accepted, all in order to make out that the ancient Egyptians were white.'[1]

This notion of a great and highly civilised African past was destined, as we shall see, to become an article of faith with many Caribbean intellectuals.

In 1927 there appeared a book which was to have a deep and lasting influence on Haitian literature, indeed on Haitian culture in general: Jean Price-Mars's *Ainsi parla l'oncle* (Port-au-Prince, 1928). The object of the book (originally a series of lectures) was to revalue and rehabilitate the African elements in Haitian life and in African civilisation itself. With this object in mind, Price-Mars analyses the civilisations of Africa, the popular beliefs, customs, and rituals of the Haitian masses of African origin. With regard to literature, he attacks the nineteenth-century writers who despised their own country, and suggests as literary material the life, customs, folk-tales and religious beliefs of the Haitian people, 'magnificent human material of which is made the warm heart, the multiple consciousness, the collective soul, of the Haitian people'.[2] In his final chapter (originally a lecture given in 1922) he makes the following protest:

> Ah, my friends, my heart is not great enough to contain all the love I feel for all men. Therefore I have no room for hatred. But I cannot prevent myself from shuddering with horror at the thought of the carnage and destruction wrought both here and in Africa with implacable method by those who boast a superior humanity and who dare now to reproach the black race with its savagery and the instability of its institutions.[3]

And he ends his chapter with the following words, 'But what were those nations and peoples which today are rotten with ostentation, prejudice and hatred, when for nineteen centuries there flourished a magnificent civilisation on the banks of the Nile? What were they? Miserable barbarians, history replies.'

The importance of Price-Mars's book is that it first set the tone of Haitian writing for his generation. Haitian writers interested themselves in their own and African folk-lore, in Haitian music and dancing; and an attitude of challenge and defiance is evinced by many—of defiance as coloured writers facing a hostile or scornful world.

A similar line is taken in the writings of the Jamaican, Marcus Garvey: Africa was cultured and civilised when Europe was still living in a state of barbarism and savagery. With Garvey, the expression is more aggressive:

> When Europe was inhabited by a race of cannibals, a race of savages, naked men, heathens and pagans, Africa was peopled by a race of men who were cultured and refined etc. Black men, you were once great; you shall be great again.[4]

Or again in one of his poems:

> Out of cold old Europe these white men came,
> From caves, dens and holes, without any fame.

> Eating their dead's flesh and sucking their blood,
> Relics of the Mediterranean flood.[5]

The idea of the past greatness of Africa is a common theme and appears in much of the writing in West Indian literature which concerns itself with Africa, although not always in the form of such incisive affirmations of African cultural superiority. Often the tone is one of nostalgia, sadness and regret, as in the following poem by the Haitian, Regnor C. Bernard, 'The Fall':

> Gone are the forests where sang and danced
> the inspired priestess,
> and the hearth of the household gods is no longer lit;
> the sacred adder sleeps no more on the mapou branch;
> the crocodiles are dead on the river banks;
> profaned are the altars of the eternal lamp;
> and the Sphinx mourns at the empty desert's edge.
> The Pharaohs are troubled at the heart of the Pyramids;
> and Africa no longer is:
> neither its temples
> nor its mysteries,
> for the priests are dead,
> for the traders in Negroes have come,
> and the tribes of the Congo, of Dahomey and the Aradas
> have known the bite of chains
> and of the whip
> and the strangling heat of drifting holds. . . .
>
> And now, only,
> in the night and the silence of the St. Domingue mountains,
> a timid throb of the drum still sometimes tries
> to raise
> up to the stars
> the profound nostalgia of the transplanted ones of Africa.[6]

One form of the rejection of European culture presents itself in the feeling that the Negro writer is somehow constrained, forced to mould his life to models which do not suit him. He is cramped and uncomfortable in his European clothes, language and patterns of thought. In a well-known poem, 'Betrayal', from his *Musique nègre* (1931), the Haitian poet Léon Laleau complains of the inadequacy of French to express his primitive soul:

> And this despair, equal to no other
> for taming, with words from France,
> this heart which came to me from Senegal.[7]

And similarly Claude McKay in 'Outcast':

> For the dim regions whence my fathers came
> My spirit, bondaged by the body, longs.
> Words felt, but never heard, my lips would frame;
> My soul would sing forgotten jungle songs.
> I would go back to darkness and to peace,
> But the great western world holds me in fee,
> And I may never hope for full release
> While to its alien gods I bend my knee.
> Something in me is lost, forever lost,
> Some vital thing has gone out of my heart,
> And I must walk the way of life a ghost
> Among the sons of earth, a thing apart.
> For I was born, far from my native clime,
> Under the white man's menace, out of time.[8]

And is it not possible to see in the use of Creole by some Haitian writers a certain distaste for the language of the white man? There are certainly other reasons for using Creole, as it is the language of the immense majority of the Haitian people, but in some writers its use seems to be connected with the complex of the rejection of Europe. This is quite clearly stated by Frank Fouché in a Creole number of the review *Optique* (no. 5, 1954):

> Creole is for black people
> Creole is for the people
> Creole is for silly Negroes who cannot
> Read or write
> Creole is for black people
> market people
> people of the coast
> people from the country parts
> Creole is not for the bourgeois.
>                    (Original written in Creole.)

The French Guianese writer, Léon Damas, in his *Pigments* (Paris, 1937) expresses this idea of discomfort much more completely in his poem 'Wages':

> I feel ridiculous
> in their shoes, in their dress suits,
> in their starched shirts, in their hard collars,
> in their monocles and bowler hats.

And from habits of dress he denounces habits of thought:

> I feel ridiculous
> with their theories which they season
> according to their needs and their passions
>
> .    .    .    .    .
>
> I feel ridiculous
> among them, an accomplice, among them a pimp,
> among them a murderer, my hands terrifyingly red
> with the blood of their civilisation.[9]

From Martinique, in Aimé Césaire's *Cahier d'un retour au pays natal* (Paris, 1947) we find the following:

> Listen to the white world
> horribly tired from its immense effort,
> hear its rebellious joints cracking under the hard stars,
> its blue steel stiffness piercing the mystical flesh,
> hear its victories trumpeting its defeats,
> hear its miserable stumbling accompanied by grandiose alibis,
> pity for our conquerors, omniscient and naïve.[10]

And from his *Soleil cou-coupé* (Paris, 1948) in the poem 'Aux écluses du vide' we find a rejection of Europe, violent and vituperative:

Europe
I give my support to all that powders the sky with its insolence
to all that is loyal and fraternal to all that has the courage to be eternally
new to all that can give its heart to fire to all that has the strength to
burst from an inexhaustible sap to all that is calm and sure
to all that is not you
Europe
pompous name for excrement.[11]

In another poem, 'Sainement', published in the literary magazine *La Trouée*, the Haitian, Philippe Thoby Marcellin, expresses himself full of a fierce joy:

> Swearing an eternal scorn for the refinements of Europe,
> I want henceforth to sing of you, revolutions, shootings, massacres,
> sound of cocomacaques on black shoulders,
> call of the lambi, mystical sensuality of voodoo,
> to sing you in a delirium three times lyrical and mystic.
> To strip off your classical trimmings

and stand up naked, very savage and very much the son of slaves
to sing in a new voice the de profundis
of your rotting civilisations.[12]

The passages quoted so far suggest a dissatisfaction with
European culture, a repugnance for its formulae of thought and
life, which are felt to limit and constrict. Naturally, in rejecting
Europe, something must take its place. What in fact takes the
place of Europe is Africa, or at least the coloured world whether
in Africa or coloured America. Some writers are very explicit
about what they find in Africa which is preferable to European
culture. In the passage already quoted Aimé Césaire denounces
Europe as being exhausted and tired with its own efforts. His
attack is clearly on European technological civilisation. Against
this, in the same poem, he puts the spirit of Africa and the
Negroes:

> Hurrah for those who have never invented anything
> for those who have never explored anything
> for those who have never tamed anything
>
> but they give themselves up, entranced, to the essence of all things
> ignorant of surfaces, but gripped by the movement of all things
> not caring to tame, but playing the game of the world
> true elder sons of the world. . . .[13]

The suggestion here is clearly that the coloured world, and
Africa in particular, has preserved a sense of the life of the earth
which has been lost in over-sophisticated European culture.
In his poem 'We Negroes', the Haitian, Jacques Lenoir, says
virtually the same thing:

> We have not colonised Africa,
> We have not discovered America
> We who are the colour of Satan.
>
> .   .   .   .   .
>
> We rise up and our dance
> is the earth turning
> our singing breaks the glasses of silence
> it is the nameless rhythm of the seasons,
> the cross roads of the four elements.[14]

Writing in the following number of the same review, *Optique*,
we find an article by Joseph D. Baguidy 'The Awakening of

Black Africa', in which the author discusses a statement of Jomo Kenyatta to the effect that black civilisation is superior to white, which is self-destructive and produces frustration and unhappiness. 'From this point of view', Baguidy writes, 'black civilisation, more human and less mechanical, which develops according to natural patterns with its own possibilities and which only cares at present for the perfection of the human personality, black civilisation is, we think, superior to white civilisation.'[15] The line of attack appears then, quite clearly, to be that European or 'white' civilisation is over-mechanised, over-sophisticated, dehumanising. The reflection of the over-sophistication of Europe is clearly expressed in the following two poems by Léon Damas, both from *Pigments*:

> Certainly.
> Then I'll put your feet in the plate
> and grab you by the scruff of the neck
> with everything that disgusts me
> in block capitals
> colonisation
> civilisation
> assimilation and the rest.[16]

And in 'Limbo':

> Give them back to me, my black dolls, so I may play with them,
> the naïve games of my instinct
> stay in the shadow of its laws
> recover my courage
> my daring,
> feel myself again,
> new self which I was yesterday,
> yesterday,
>        without complexity
>            yesterday
> at the time of the up-rooting.[17]

In Joan Brièrre's *Le drapeau de demain*, a dramatic poem in two acts, in which the souls of Dessalines and Geffrard rise and express their horror and disappointment at what has happened to Haiti since independence, 'civilisation' is attacked for having produced slavery and encouraged racial discrimination:

> Men lead by the low instincts of beasts,
> and draping themselves in the vain name of civilisers,

and believing themselves the kings of the whole planet,
command that the Negro, branded by his colour,
throughout the world, should be an unconscious thing,
a stepping stone for their ostentation,
should live in the night, and die in filth
while Civilisation, carrying its torch
stained with the blood of our race,
watches them parade under triumphal arches.[18]

In the Haitian review *Les Griots* (1938-1939), the case of African civilisation is put very forcibly. Carl Brouard, writing in the first number under the title of 'Doctrine of the New School' says: 'The abolished splendours of the civilisations of the Sudan made our hearts bleed'. And in the second number, Lorimer Denis and François Duvalier, in an article entitled 'The Essentials of the Doctrine of the Griots', state that 'The Haitian élite rejects the primordial factor in our civilisation to the exclusive benefit of the Gallo-Latin influence. Hence our moral unbalance, logically leading to the American occupation.'[19] They continue: 'Since on the one hand all our efforts since Independence to this day have consisted in the systematic repression of our African heritage, in the literary and the political and social fields, our action should lead us to demand the revaluation of this racial factor.'[20] And they end by claiming an 'integral reform of Haitian mentality' based on both factors, the European and the African, but principally the African, which had hitherto been neglected. The same two writers in a subsequent number of the review *Les Griots*, in an article on 'Ethnical and Historical Psychology', have the following to say:

Voodoo is not a product of magic and gross superstition. Worked out on the land of Africa, whose powerful mystery it reflects, a product of spirituality going back to a legendary past, voodoo is none the less the expression of a race before the riddles of this world. Voodoo is essentially cosmogonic, philosophical and spiritualist.[21]

The defence and idealisation of the civilisations of Africa has indeed become almost a commonplace of the works of many West Indian writers. In *Discourse on Colonialism* (Paris, 1950) a political pamphlet which reads more like a poem in its emotionalism and rhythm, Aimé Césaire attacks the barbarism of European colonisation, accusing the Europeans of having been savage, cruel and callous. Many of the primitive societies broken up by the coming of the Europeans in Africa were happy and balanced. 'They were common-holding societies, never societies of all for a few. They were not only pre-capitalist but anti-capitalist. They were democratic communities. They were co-operative fraternal communities. I make a systematic apologia of societies destroyed by imperialism.'[22] He goes on to point out that for material progress Europeanisation was not essential, and quotes the example of Japan. The following passage is worth quoting in its entirety, as it touches the very heart of the problem:

> The Viet-Namese, before the arrival of the French in their country, were a people of an ancient, exquisite and refined culture. We must not remind the Bank of Indo-China. Turn on the forgetting machine.
> The men of Madagascar who are being tortured today were, less than a century ago, poets, artists, administrators. But silence. Button up your mouth.
> Fortunately there were the Negroes. The Negroes. Well, let's talk about the Negroes. Let's talk about them.
> What about the Sudanese empire? The bronzes of Benin? Shongo sculpture? Fair enough. All that will not change the lamentable and sensational baubles which adorn so many European capitals. And African music. Why not?

And he finishes:

> Civilised to the marrow of their bones. The idea of the barbarous Negro is a European idea.[23]

The idea that Africa possesses, or that Africa possessed in the past, civilisations of great splendour and refinement is found very frequently. It is often coupled with the idea that the white man, the European, destroyed African civilisation in his lust for wealth and power. Although these writings which praise African civilisations, even if they are of the past and have ceased to be, do not state a direct rejection of European culture, they certainly represent an implied criticism, inasmuch as they point to the brutal and barbarous destruction at the period of the slave-trade.

Another avenue of attack on European civilisation consists in a criticism of Christianity in its relation to the Negro world. The line taken is a fairly obvious one that Christianity is at best a white man's religion, closing its eyes to racial discrimination and indifferent to the oppression and persecution of the Negro, and at worst, an active agent of colonialism helping to keep the Negro in subjection. The attacks range from mildly ironical remarks like the following quotation from the Martinican writer, Mayotte Capécia, in *Je suis martiniquaise*: 'No doubt the God that Father Labbat revealed to my ancestors is also the God of coloured people, but he is still white',[24] to the violent anti-clericalism of Jacques Roumain, Paul Niger, Aimé Césaire, etc.

A poem from Roumain's *Bois d'ébène* (Port-au-Prince, 1945, dated Brussels, 1939), 'The New Negro Sermon', is anti-clerical and I think fundamentally anti-Christian. It uses a Christian background and set of references to increase its emotional force. The theme of the poem is that 'they', that is 'the rich men, the Pharisees, the landowners and bankers', have defiled and degraded the Negro. Christ today is in the house of the thieves, the Church preaches submission to the rich, and in the cellars of the monasteries the servants of the Church hoard their wealth. Roumain uses a number of Biblical phrases, twisting them to his purpose, but they nevertheless retain much of their emotional force by association. For example:

> We shall not forgive them, for they know what they do.
>
> .    .    .    .    .
>
> They have made of the bleeding man the bloody god.
> Oh Judas snigger, snigger Judas.
>
> .    .    .    .    .
>
> In the cellars of the monasteries the priest counts the
> interest on the thirty pieces of silver.

The poem ends with a complete rejection of Christianity:

> No brothers, comrades,
> We shall pray no more
>
> .    .    .    .    .
>
> We shall no longer sing our sad despairing spirituals.
> Another song shall surge from our throats,
> and we shall unfurl our red banners.[25]

In another poem, 'Dirty Niggers', from the same book we find an even more violent and abusive rejection of Christianity:

> Surprise
> Jesus Mary Joseph
> when we catch the missionary by the beard

> laughing horribly
> to teach him in our turn
> by kicking his bottom
> that our ancestors were not Gauls,
> and that we don't give a damn
> for a God who,
> if he is the father,
> well, we, the dirty niggers,
> it is obvious that we must be his bastard sons,
> and it won't help yelling
> Jesus Mary Joseph
> like an old bladder spilling over with lies. . . .[26]

The manner of this writing is vituperative, intentionally disrespectful of established Christian values, and again quite intentionally shocking, or intended to shock. The Guadeloupe writer Paul Niger, in his poem 'Je n'aime pas l'Afrique', uses a similar technique of heavy sarcasm plus coarse and vulgar argot, which he makes God speak. The following is one of the milder passages of the poem.

> Christ redeemed sinful man and built his Church in Rome.
> His voice was heard in the desert. The Church on top of Society
> and Society on top of the Church, the one carrying the other
> founded civilisation where men, docile to the ancient wisdom
> to appease the old gods, not dead,
> sacrifice every ten years several million victims.
>
> He had forgotten Africa.
> But it was noticed that a race (of men?)
> still had not paid God its tribute of black blood, they reminded him
> So Jesus spread his hands over the curly heads, and the Negroes were
>   saved.
> Not in this world, of course.[27]

At another level, although essentially following the same line, is René Piquion's book, *Langston Hughes: A New Song*, a partial biography of Langston Hughes with French translations of his poems. The work contains a number of attacks on Christianity, for example: 'And to make them (the Negroes) for ever submissive, in the days of slavery and in capitalist society, they are served with the classical medicine, of subtle and reliable effects—religious opium. The cross always precedes or accompanies the gun.'[28] And even more violent and fundamental (an attack at once on the Church and also quite explicitly on western European civilisation):

> The hand raised in blessing absolves in advance all the crimes perpetuated in the name of Christian civilisation, the injustices of soulless capitalism. The Church teaches the curly, bent heads, with an unsurpassable perfidiousness, the comforting art of resignation on earth, in the hope one day of enjoying, beyond the empty tomb, an infinite beatitude. In their deep distress, aggravated by their ignorance of the causes of their misfortunes, the Negroes resort to mystical illusions.[29]

So we see at least four main lines of attack or rejection.

First, the feeling that the Caribbean Negro is somehow constricted in the moulds of European thought and behaviour patterns which are not fitted to his nature. Linked with this is the interest in African cultures, past and present, both in Africa and their remains in the West Indies. Second, the feeling that European civilisation has failed, by becoming excessively concerned with power and technical progress and not sufficiently concerned with the production of happiness for the human individual. African or Negro culture is presented as being nearer to nature and nearer to man. Third, the rejection of Christianity as an agent or ally of colonialism; and finally, the attack on European civilisation for the brutality and cynicism with which it enslaved and exploited the Negro, while still maintaining high-sounding principles of freedom and humanitarianism.

Historically, the period at which these attitudes appear in Caribbean literature is certainly between 1920 and 1960, and this period can be further narrowed to 1925–1960. That is to say that the period in which these attitudes are developed coincides with certain contemporary political and aesthetic trends. Anti-imperialism of the Marxist variety was particularly fashionable in left- and extreme left-wing intellectual circles in Europe in the years immediately following the First World War, and French radical anti-imperialism was invariably accompanied by strong anti-clericalism, which indeed is part and parcel of French radicalism in general. It is significant that the most violent expressions of rejection of Christianity come from writers (from Haiti, and the French West Indies) who are all closely connected with Paris as an intellectual centre. Brierre, Roumain, Césaire have all spent considerable periods of time in Paris, where they have opportunities of meeting French African intellectuals thinking along similar lines. The attack on European civilisation, and particularly on Christianity, can, then, quite clearly be seen in the context of radical or Marxist European thought of the 1920–40 period.

Another influence which certainly should be taken into account is a semi-aesthetic one, i.e. the whole complex of iconoclasm which came to a head in the Surrealism of the 1920s. The revaluation of primitive art had started much earlier with the Cubists and the fashion for Negro art in the period 1900–20. Writing of this period Georges Lemaître says:

> The candid expression of genuine, though brutal, sensations and sentiments, stirred man in a way that was beyond the power of a clever, sophisticated technique. So it became obvious that the hard crust of an age-old civilisation, the thick layer of interpretative notions and traditions which intelligence had deposited upon all things, was the main obstacle to direct contact with the richest sources of human inspiration and emotion.[30]

This movement towards primitivism developed in the 1920s into a powerful vogue for Negro sculpture, music (mainly in the form of jazz), and a preoccupation with the organisation of primitive societies. Dadaism and its successor Surrealism were the enemies of all traditional notions of art and indeed of all that was regarded as the European cultural heritage. They made a systematic onslaught on all established values whether in art, literature, morals, religion or politics. Like the Marxist radicals, they were violently anti-clerical and indeed anti-Christian. They not only questioned but jeered destructively and used every form of weapon from caricature and satire to virulent and obscene abuse, to shatter acquired, traditional responses. Anything 'primitive' appealed greatly to the Surrealists, as it was not associated with the odious superconsciousness of traditional European culture which they regarded as having been wrong from the start. Both Communists and Surrealists made it their mission to attack and demolish all that pertained to 'decadent' or *bourgeois* culture. It is not surprising that young colonial intellectuals should have drawn lessons from all this. Roumain was a Communist in politics and owes much to Surrealism for his literary technique; Aimé Césaire was for many years a Communist in politics (he has represented Martinique as a Communist deputy) and a declared Surrealist in his writing. The intellectual background of such writers as Brierre, Zobel, Damas and Niger is clearly very radical.

Apart from the Communist and left-wing attacks on decadent *bourgeois* culture, we find an attack from another quarter—the Fascists; also, as we have seen, there was the considerable influence of Oswald Spengler, whose *Decline of the West* was widely and avidly read in America. The initiator of the Afro-Caribbean movement, the Puerto Rican, Luis Palés Matos, had the following to say in an article which appeared in the magazine *Poliedro* (San Juan, 1927) and which has already been quoted but is worth quoting again here:

> The aesthetic sense of the white race has reached a stage of dangerous cerebralisation, cutting itself off from its cosmic roots. I do not believe in a monumental art of purely cerebral representation; I only believe in an art which identifies itself with the thing and fuses with the essence of the thing.

And after talking about art being the outcome of 'the urge of the blood', he goes on to quote Spengler on the 'metaphysical' decadence of contemporary European art. And he concludes: 'The super-literariness from which the Western world suffers is an unmistakable symptom of decadence.'[31] So, like Spengler, he sees Europe as exhausted and as having worked out all its artistic possibilities, and he even speaks of 'the progressive and wilful sterility of the white race'.

If these quotations are not sufficient to prove the Spenglerian influence on Palés Matos and the Afro-Antillianism of Puerto Rico and Cuba, here is another quotation from an article published on the death of Spengler, in *El Mundo* (San Juan), by Juan Antonio Corretjer. It is called 'Spengler—a Creole Projection':

> That Spengler was the intellectual apostle of the appearance of the Negro in the artistic hemisphere of Europe, there is no doubt. The apogee of the Negro, as an artistic novelty, follows on the appearance of Spengler's theories. Palés read and for a time was under the spell of Spengler.[32]

If other writers of the Afro-Antillian movement of the 1930s— such as the Cubans Guillén, Ballagas, Carpentier, Guirao, etc.— were not exactly under the spell of Spengler, their super-evaluation of the primitive elements in Caribbean life certainly has its distant roots in Spengler's theories of Western cultural exhaustion.

One other point is worth mentioning, and that is the political and cultural awakening of Africa, particularly of black Africa. During this period there grew up among coloured people all over the world who were suffering from some form of colonialism, exploitation or discrimination on racial grounds a feeling of community. Many West Indian intellectuals who met African writers and thinkers in Paris and London developed an interest in African culture whose values were being brought to the fore by African writers. This explains why many of them, when they started to think in terms of a culture of their own, a culture which was not just an adaptation of that which they received from Europe, turned to Africa. Africa seems to exercise a powerful fascination over many West Indian intellectuals. The fascination is largely emotional and political, although serious attempts to get to know about Africa and to learn more about African elements in Caribbean life have been made. The review *Les Griots* (1938-39) in Haiti, the *Bureau d'Etudes Ethnographiques* (founded by Jacques Roumain in 1941), the *Revista de Estudios Afrocubanos* (1939-40) are significant in this respect.

The strongest and most fundamental attack on European civilisation has come from writers in the Caribbean territories which are under French cultural influence. The Jamaican, Claude McKay, for instance, although he felt very deeply the predicament of the Negro and although in the poem quoted in this chapter he seems to hanker after a means of expression more akin to his nature, made no wholesale rejection either of Christianity or of European cultural values in general, and in fact did not accept the overtures of the Communists who went to considerable lengths to win him over.

In Cuba and Puerto Rico, although we find anti-imperialism as a very common theme in poetry, novels and short stories and also a great interest in the Negro elements in Cuban life amounting in the period 1926-40 to a veritable literary fashion, there is no direct rejection of the traditions of European culture and civilisation, only an attempt to find a distinctive Cuban tonality in the concert of world culture, which is not the same thing at all. The same is true of the Dominican Republic, where fear of Haitian infiltration over the frontier has driven the Dominican Government into a position of strong support for all that is most Spanish, i.e. most European, in their cultural life. Measures have been

taken to eradicate any traces of Haitian influence either in language, customs or religious practices (voodoo) from the frontier
provinces. Here is a most categorical affirmation of European
values and rejection of the 'African' values of Haiti. Joaquín
Balaguer writes:

> If the immense majority of the Dominican population were to be African-
> ised, as it would be Africanised if no measures were taken to prevent it, Haiti,
> whose policies have always been fanatically racialist, would in the more or
> less near future, realise its old dream of the indivisibility of the island.[33]

The critical attitude towards the traditional culture of Europe
on the part of West Indian (and African) writers has attracted
considerable attention to Europe itself. In the last twelve years
two important anthologies have been published: *Nouvelle
anthologie de la poésie nègre et malgache*, selected by the French
African writer Léopold Sédar Senghor, with a long preface,
*l'Orphée noir*, by Jean-Paul Sartre (Paris, 1948) and *Schwarzer
Orpheus*—modern poems by African peoples in both hemi-
spheres, translated into German and selected by Janheinz Jahn
(Munich, 1954). The bulk of the poems in both collections is from
the West Indies.

One of the reasons why European intellectuals are so fascinated
by the critique of European culture by West Indian and African
writers is that the attack has come just at a moment when western
Europe is unsure of itself. It is not that Europe has not become
quite accustomed to cries about its own decadence. The French
symbolists and English writers of 1890 luxuriated in the idea of
their 'decadence' and the 'Noble Savage' goes back at least to the
Renaissance. However, the First World War, the Nazi-Fascist
period, the Second World War, the growth of Communism and
the threat of another war, all these have severely shaken that confidence and optimism which were at the very heart of European
culture. Unlimited confidence and optimism in its own potentialities of development have been, indeed, the basis of European
civilisation since the Renaissance. Any change was to be change
for the better. The French *Encyclopédistes* of the eighteenth
century rejected the *ancien régime* but were confident in a new
and better order of things. The social idealism of the nineteenth
century, from Fourier to the English Fabians, was confident of a
better future. Today, however, Europe has the feeling that the

reins of its future are no longer even in its own hands. And at this moment it has to face an attack from outside. Europe is being looked at and judged—critically. Sartre puts this very pointedly in his essay *l'Orphée noir*. 'Here are black men', he writes, 'who are standing up and looking at us—I hope you feel, like I do, the thrill of being looked at. For the white man has enjoyed for three thousand years the privilege of looking without being looked at.'[34]

# CHAPTER IV

# THE FRENCH WEST INDIAN
# BACKGROUND OF *NÉGRITUDE*

THE word *négritude* appeared for the first time in print in a long poem by the Martinican, Aimé Césaire, in *Cahier d'un retour au pays natal* (Paris, 1947). Subsequently the word has come into common use in the discussion of neo-African literature and art. It is to be seen frequently in the pages of such literary reviews as *Présence Africaine* and *Black Orpheus*. The concept of *négritude* has also been analysed at considerable length by such writers as J.-P. Sartre, in his *l'Orphée noir*[1] and more recently by Janheinz Jahn in *Muntu.*[2]

Césaire's poem not only contains the first use of the word, but it supplies a brief picture of the various stages of the development of the concept. For this reason it may be worth while, at this stage, to give a brief summary of the poem. The poem starts with a blisteringly bitter evocation of the poverty, decay and hopelessness of colonial Martinique—a tremendous, inspired wave of disgust envelops everything. This passes into an expression of hate for the white world, symbolised in the 'white' death of Toussaint L'Ouverture in his prison in the snow-bound Jura, and develops into an attack on reason. In this revolt against reason, Césaire turns to primitivism, magic and iconoclasm (considered from a European point of view):

> Because we hate you and your reason, and we turn to
> the precocious dementia of flaming madness
> of persistent cannibalism.[3]

This wallowing in hatred, unreason, in the rejection of European values and in self-humiliation, is resolved, however, into something positive. Through his suffering and abasement, the Negro (Césaire speaks for all Negroes) has learned something. In his apparent negativeness, again from a European point of view, he possesses something of great value which the over-mechanised

European has either forgotten or lost. Once again it is worth repeating a quotation, this time more fully:

> Hurrah for those who have never invented anything
> for those who have never explored anything
> for those who have never tamed anything
>
> but they give themselves up, entranced, to the essence of all things
> ignorant of surfaces, but gripped by the movement of all things
> not caring to tame, but playing the game of the world
>
> truly the elder sons of the earth
> open to all the breaths of the world
> brotherly space for the breaths of the world
> river-bed without drainage for all the waters of the world
> spark of the sacred fire of the world
> flesh of the flesh of the world alive with the movement of the world.[4]

And it is precisely this mystical oneness with the world which the 'white world' has lost:

> Listen to the white world
> horribly weary from its immense effort,
> hear its rebellious joints cracking under
> the hard stars,
> its blue steel stiffness piercing
> the mystical flesh. . . .
>
> pity for our conquerors, omniscient and naïve.[5]

With this knowledge, the tone of the poem changes, for this awareness of his value, and his values, has permitted him to shake off the old shamefaced *négritude*. There is pride and an immense hope, for the work of man is not finished, but has only just begun, and the Negro is on his feet and free, ready to make his own contribution in his own terms. It should be emphasised that this newly found freedom is a *result* of the discovery of the Negro modality, of *négritude*, and this is brought out quite clearly in the poem. Besides the quotations already given, which point clearly enough the direction of the poet's thought, he states his position quite unequivocally in the following passage:

> my *négritude* is not a stone, its deafness thrown up against the clamour of
> the day,
> my *négritude* is not a pool of dead water on the dead eye of the earth

my *négritude* is not a tower nor a cathedral
it delves into the red flesh of the soil
it plunges into the burning flesh of the sky.[6]

It is, then, a sort of telluric mysticism discovered by the Negro as a result of being rejected as inferior by the white world, which considers that at best he can learn the ways of white civilisation. In a brilliant analysis of the position of the Negro *vis-à-vis* white civilisation a compatriot of Césaire Frantz Fanon makes the same point, perhaps with less dramatic force, but with greater clarity, in his *Peau noire masques blancs*:

The scientists... have admitted that the Negro is a human creature: physically and mentally he has developed analogously to the white man, the same morphology, the same histology. On all fronts reason has secured our victory. But this very victory was making a fool of me. In theory it was agreed: the Negro is a human being. But what good was that to me? Too late. Between them and me stood a world—the white world. For they were not capable of wiping out the past.[7]

I had rationalised my environment, but it had rejected me in the name of colour prejudice. Since there was no understanding on the basis of reason, I threw myself into the arms of the irrational. I became irrational up to my neck. The tom-tom drummed out my cosmic mission. The arteries of the world, torn open, made me fertile. I found, not my origin, but *the* origin. The white man has never understood this magical substitution. He desires the world and wants it for himself alone. He considers himself predestined to rule the world. He has made it useful to himself. But there are values which do not submit to his rule. Like a sorcerer I steal from the white man a certain world which he cannot identify.[8]

And to complete the similarity with Césaire's poetised account of *négritude* he observes: 'As an American friend of mine said to me, I had become in the mechanised world of the white man the guardian of humanity.'[9]

The context, then, quite clearly, consists of the Negro's revolt against the position of inferiority assigned to him; against his economic exploitation; a criticism and rejection of 'white' values and the propounding of an attitude to life and a way of apprehending reality which are quite different (the difference is constantly stressed) and specifically Negro, belonging to Negroes the world over. The approach to life through *négritude* is felt to be somehow richer, more natural, and there is the suggestion that white civilisation has gone wrong and has taken, from a human point of view, a wrong turning into excessive materialism, pragmatism and technomania.

In art and literature, as would be expected, *négritude* involves a radically new approach. Art does not operate through reason or logic, but through magic, through fascination. It is a possession and recreation of the world through the magic power of the word. Some critics were deceived into thinking that the products of *négritude* were Surrealist, and, indeed, it was André Breton, the high-priest of Surrealism, who took up Césaire, and to some extent launched him. However, in spite of superficial resemblances, on closer inspection it is quite clear that *négritude* is different from Surrealism. Puzzled by the true nature of *négritude*, Sartre in his *l'Orphée noir*,[10] where he deals with the subject on a metaphysical level, is forced into the paradox of describing *négritude* as a 'committed, even directed, automatic writing'. And yet, this is perhaps the best way of accounting for the practices of *négritude* writers, for while there is a deliberate subject, theme or purpose, the artist abandons himself to it with complete creative freedom. Indeed, this is the very essence of *négritude* in art. As Césaire puts it in his *Les armes miraculeuses* :

> Out of the sky, the birds, the parrots, the bells, silk cloth and drums, out of a touch of drunkenness and wild endearments, out of copper clanging and mother-of-pearl, out of Sundays, dancing, children's words, and love words, out of love for the little fists of children, I will build a world, my world with round shoulders.[11]

It should be pointed out here, however, that the aesthetic aspect of *négritude* as a sort of directed Surrealism is found, at least in French West Indian writers, almost exclusively in Césaire, and, as we shall see later, it is the programmatic features of *négritude* which predominate. This does not mean to say that what Césaire and Fanon claim for *négritude* does not apply to some African expressions of the Negro way of art both in English and French.[12]

So *négritude* appears today as a formulation of a Negro attitude to life and to art. It has been analysed and interpreted as a philosophy by Sartre and in terms of traditional African (Bantu) values, as Nonno, by Janheinz Jahn,[13] Nonno being the magic procreative power of the word. And yet, although since 1945 *négritude* has been given a pan-Negro and fundamentally African context, largely as the result of the collaboration and mixing of

African and French West Indian writers in French intellectual circles, it still retains, at least historically, a West Indian connexion, and although it is possible to see in the poems of Césaire a synthesis of historical *négritude*, at least in its main features, it may be useful to look at the various and gradual stages through which *négritude* passed before becoming susceptible to a clear and definite formulation such as we have seen in Césaire and Fanon.

From its very beginnings, *négritude* has moved in a French atmosphere, and it is to the ex-French colony of Haiti that one must look to find its roots. Perhaps the first stirrings do not appear to bear much resemblance to the fully-fledged formulation we have seen in Césaire and Fanon, but in Haiti is to be found the first awareness, the first *prise de conscience*, of the Negro in a white world, and it is the unbroken continuity of the theme in Haitian literature that forces the conclusion that to a very large extent, historically, the concept of *négritude* grew out of the Haitian situation. After Haiti became independent in 1804 the French cultural link was not broken. Indeed, to Haitian thinkers of the nineteenth century, culture and civilisation were essentially French: *French* culture, *French* civilisation, and while the subjects of their writing remained Haitian to a large extent (the struggle for freedom against a background of slavery, the epic fight for independence, the great figures of the period of independence—Christophe, Dessalines, Toussaint L'Ouverture—and Haitian landscape) the literary ideals of the Haitian intelligentsia were French. French political dominion may have been repudiated, French literary fashions were certainly not. In the midst of this cultural Francophilia, the idea that independent 'black' Haiti had the historical mission of demonstrating to the world the capacity for 'civilisation' (*à la française*) of a coloured people of African descent was not slow in making its appearance. While much was published along these lines between 1850 and 1900, two works stand out as clear formulations of this trend: Anténor Firmin's *De l'égalité des races humaines* (Paris, 1885) and Hannibal Price's *De la réhabilitation de la race noire par le peuple d'Haïti* (Paris, 1900). In *De l'égalité des races humaines* Firmin points to the achievements of ancient Egyptian civilisation, and quotes travellers on the beauty and organisation of Sudanese cities to refute the idea of the Negro's cultural incapacity. Haiti, he thinks, has a special role: 'to show the whole world that all men, black or white, are equal in qualities as they are equal in rights'.[14] He also considers that Haiti should serve as an example for the 'rehabilitation of Africa'.[15]

Taking up the theme of the rehabilitation of the black race *by the Haitian people*, Hannibal Price stresses even more strongly the part played by Haiti in restoring the dignity of the Negro in the world. The following quotation states this view very forcibly:

> I am a man of Haiti, the Mecca, the Judea of the black race, the country where are to be found the sacred fields of Vertières, la Crête à Pierrot, la Ravine aux Couleuvres, le Tombeau des Indigènes [scenes of battles in the Haitian war of independence], and a hundred others where every man with African blood in his veins should go on a pilgrimage at least once in his life, for it was there that the Negro became a man: it was there, that, breaking his chains, he condemned slavery in the New World for ever.[16]

It is apparent, however, in his discussion of voodoo practices of African origin, that he rejects these as signs of backwardness which lead foreigners to scorn Haiti for its primitiveness. The people of Haiti, he affirms, are profoundly attached to Christianity. The book also contains a spirited attack on racial prejudice, very suggestive in tone and general direction of subsequent onslaughts on colonialism. 'Racial prejudice', he writes, 'ceases to be an error and becomes a crime when it is deliberately used to perpetuate inequality by falsifying institutions and customs. The formula is: the conquered are inferior, therefore they must remain inferior.'[17] And again: 'Colour prejudice is the work of the white man. Whatever form it assumes, whatever its gradations may be, it is the work of the white man, coldly calculated, deliberately applied, by the white man for his profit and exclusive benefit.'[18] There is no doubt that the tone and import of these two books are very close to the expression of *négritude* in such contemporary writers as Aimé Césaire, Jacques Roumain, Paul Niger, Frantz Fanon and others. It is true that both authors are still trying to justify the Negro and his civilisation in terms of European culture (the cultures of ancient Egypt and the Sudan are compared favourably with those of Greece and Rome; charges of primitivism, because of voodoo, are rejected) but the insistence on the place in the world of the Negro, as a cultural equal, the denunciation of colour prejudice as a cunning trick to perpetuate inequalities, the revaluation of African cultures—all these features relate the work of Firmin and Price to the current of *négritude*.

Although in a lighter vein, the tendency of Haitian poets of the nineteenth century to praise the beauty of black women can be seen as part of the same trend—the total reappraisal of the Negro. This also figures prominently in the *négritude* writers of the 1940s and 1950s (Léon Damas, Lionel Attuly, Philippe Thoby Marcellin, Jacques Stéphen Alexis etc.). 'No race has the monopoly of beauty, intelligence or strength', writes Césaire in his *Cahier*.[19]

The next important milestone in the development of *négritude* in Haiti is Jean Price-Mars's *Ainsi parla l'oncle* (Port-au-Prince, 1928). Between 1900 and 1928, however, important changes had taken place in the cultural atmosphere of Haiti. Faith in French ways of doing things had been shaken, partly as the result of the several years of political chaos leading to the American occupation in 1915. French institutions appeared to have failed in Haiti and French culture was felt to be excessively literary. It was suggested that British and American models might be better suited to Haitian conditions. The shock caused by the American occupation in 1915 awakened an intense national feeling, but it was not to its French heritage that the Haitian intellectuals turned, but rather to the traditions of the people which, scorned and neglected for over a century, had retained many African features in its folk culture. When Price-Mars wrote in 1928: 'We have no chance of being ourselves unless we repudiate no part of our ancestral heritage. And indeed this heritage for eight-tenths of us is a gift from Africa',[20] he was voicing the new trend, and thereby becoming the guide, the *maître-à-penser* of two successive generations of Haitian intellectuals. Price-Mars urged his compatriots to look into their folklore—into the stories, legends, proverbs, religious practices, music and dancing of the Haitian people which had been ignored or scorned during the 'French' nineteenth century. He recommends the study of African civilisations and of African elements in Haitian folklore, pointing out that the mystique of Africa is still very much alive in Haitian folklore, full of references to 'Guinée'. He lashes out savagely at the racial prejudices of the Haitian *élite*, its snobbish worship of everything French or foreign, its attempts at racial and cultural dissociation from the people.

Some aspects of Price-Mars's predication affect Haiti alone, but others reach out far beyond the Haitian scene. One of his more far-reaching ideas is the importance of Africa to this West Indian society, his encouragement of the study of the African heritage and civilisations for the light they can throw on Haitian civilisation. Another idea perhaps more important in the context of *négritude* is his assumption that the Haitian has something very rare and very specific to offer the world. 'May it not be', he writes, 'that we have something to offer to the world which is not something watered down or imitated? In the accelerated speed and dryness, we shall be still, for the rest of the world one of the precious reservoirs of poetry, joy and love.'[21] Romantically, lyrically expressed, is this not a prefiguration of the very essence of *négritude*? From this point onward, the drums start to beat in the literature of Haiti. Poets express their nostalgia for the lost 'home' where they were happy, uncomplicated, where they were 'themselves'. They yearn for primitivism, to throw off the false refinements of civilisation, 'to drink blood out of human skulls'. The peasant novel starts with Jacques Roumain's *Montagne ensorcelée* (1931) and Jean-Baptiste Cinéas's *Drame de la terre* (1933), full of voodoo mysticisms, and culminates in Jacques Stéphen Alexis's *Les arbres musiciens*, where the earthy spirituality of voodoo is set up as a kind of nature-philosophy. In Jacques Roumain the brotherhood in suffering and the revolt of the Negroes of the world are ringingly proclaimed, and joined with the revolt of all the other damned ones. All these writers revel in being 'primitive', iconoclastic, in being black, anti-Christian, anti-white, although some are careful to point out that they are not racialist except in the context of a 'white civilisation' which rejects them. For example, Aimé Césaire says:

> Make not of me that man of hate, for whom I have only hatred
> although I set myself down in one single race
> you know my tyrannical love
> you know that it is not out of hate for other races
> that I demand to dig for this single race
> that what I want is for universal hunger
> for universal thirst.[22]

and Jacques Roumain in *Bois d'ébène* after a furious embittered rhapsody on the sufferings of the Negro, stops himself short with a 'POURTANT' in capital letters:

And yet,
I only want to belong to your race,
workers and peasants of all countries.[23]

The tone of impassioned vituperation against 'white' civilisation and its values is, however, prevalent. Nothing escapes the
denunciations. The Christian religion is treated as an opiate to
keep the Negro in subjection and its hypocritical connivance with
colonialism and imperialism is stressed.[24] White architecture,
clothes, music, dancing, philosophy, art—all come under the axe.
The reason for the violence of these attacks is obvious. It is a
question of undermining the tremendous prestige of 'white'
culture, which had been presented, arrogantly or paternally, to
the non-white world as the only valid culture. This phase of
vituperation appears as necessary in order to quash the feeling
of inferiority, of tutelage, of acceptance; it is not an essential
part of négritude, only a phase, though perhaps an inevitable one.
In Césaire's Cahier the tone of bitterness disappears once the
true meaning of négritude has been discovered and is replaced by
a tone of jubilation, for what most matters to the theoreticians and
practitioners of négritude is the proclamation of a set of Negro
values, cultural in the widest sense, and the universal acceptance
of these values. In another Martinican writer, Gilbert Gratiant,
négritude is proclaimed with serenity in terms similar to those
used by Césaire:

The earth is full of trees,
The sky of storms,
Water seeps from the warm soils where the animal sleeps,
And the Negro knows
From a long and intimate cousinage,
The language of the waters speaking to the stars,
The will of the wind and the orders of fire.

Thanks in the name of man,
For what you have given,
Your arms were full,
And bending your knee
Slave or warrior,
You placed at the feet of the world
The fruits of fervour and the power of rhythm.[25]

In spite, however, of the ultimate aim of négritude, the acceptance of Negro values in terms of themselves, most of the West

Indian *négritude* writers have not gone beyond the vituperative stage and continue to flagellate white civilisation and throw themselves into an exaggerated primitiveness. Indeed, there seems to be little progress either in content or style between Philippe Thoby Marcellin's poem 'Sainement' (in the Haitian review *La Trouée*, July 1927) in which the writer 'swears his eternal scorn for European refinements' and ends up 'naked, very much the descendant of slaves' intoning the requiem for rotting civilisations, Léon Damas's hate-filled diatribes in *Pigments* (Paris, 1937) and a poem by the Martinican, Georges Desportes, 'Auto da fé', dated 1944 and published in Damas's anthology *Poètes d'expression française* (Paris, 1947) in which he says:

> We have stripped off our European clothes,
> Magnificent brutes and barbarians that we are,
> And we have danced naked around the high flames—
>
> .　　.　　.　　.　　.
>
> Stark naked around the great bonfire of joy,
> Stark naked under the palm-trees, stark naked under the bamboos
> We shout under the sky of the Tropics,
> To the sound of powerful Caribbean jazz,
> Our pride in being Negroes,
> The glory of being black.[26]

Africa is certainly present in the minds of many of the French West Indian *négritude* writers, and is the theme of many of their poems. It varies from a hankering after a happy African 'primitiveness' to an identification with the sufferings and struggle of Africa under colonialism. African 'primitiveness' is conceived of by many writers in the most naïve and conventional European terms. Although much has been written about a style of *négritude*, apart from its content and attitudes, with the exception of Césaire himself it is difficult to find any style or manner in the French West Indian writers which could be described as distinctively African or un-European. Their impassioned denunciations of the white world, their nostalgia for Africa, their diatribes against racialism, paternalism and the economic extortions of the colonial powers are couched in literary terms which in spite of the subject-matter, are European or Western in the sense that they might easily have been used by any French, English, Spanish or American writer. Common features of the writing of West

Indian *négritude* writers over the last forty years have been the absence of rhyme, punctuation and often of any recognisable rhythm; the general violence of expression through the use of emotionally charged words and images, chaotic enumerations, reiteration for the sake of emotional intensification, and in some cases rhythmical nonsense words such as *batouque, voom rouh* (Césaire). Of Surrealism, even modified and utilised selectively, there is very little sign. The meaning of most of these poems is perfectly obvious; indeed many are excessively rhetorical.

*Négritude* as a set of attitudes leading to revaluation of the Negro value all over the world in the face of white civilisation appears to have started and gone through a great deal of its development in the literature of the French West Indies. It has been taken up by French African writers since 1945, but the foundations were certainly laid in Haiti and the French islands of the West Indies.

The fundamental thesis of *négritude* has been restated, very forcibly, at an abstract level by the Haitian novelist, Jacques Stéphen Alexis, in a long article 'Du réalisme merveilleux des haitiens' in *Présence Africaine* (June–November 1956), read at the First International Congress of Black Writers and Artists held in Paris in the same year.

He appears slightly critical of *négritude*, which he apparently finds in need of a clearer definition, though he considers it valuable as an antidote to the 'Haiti as a cultural province of France' theory. He sees it as 'something dynamic, and profitable to Haitian culture'. The danger of *négritude*, he points out, is that it may conceal the 'cultural autonomy of the Haitian people'. However, such mild criticisms are overshadowed by repeated reference to the African connexions in, and also the African nature of, Haitian culture. Indeed, he emphasises the African cultural heritage in Haiti, going so far as to affirm that *all* peoples who have their origins in Africa display a notable permanence of cultural features, and to claim that works of art produced by people in countries of African origin are more readily 'felt' by men of Negro origin than any other kinds of art.

The Haitian people, *like other peoples of African origins*, have a very personal vision of sensuous reality, of the movement and rhythm of life, he goes on.

Classical canons of beauty in the arts are meaningless and

savour of cultural imperialism. Haitian art, *like the art of other people of Negro origin,* is different from Western art of Graeco-Latin filiation, which tends too often to 'intellectuality, idealisation, to the creation of canons of perfection, to logical unity, to a pre-established harmony where our art tends to the exact sensuous representation of reality, to creative intuition, to character and to expressive power'. And he rounds off his study: 'Long live a living realism, tied to the magic of the universe, a realism which shakes not only the mind, but also the heart and the tree of the nerves.' He claims that the naturalness and humanism in Haitian art (as in the art of all peoples of Negro origin) lead always towards man in contrast with the 'intellectualist constructions of the decadent West with its cold-blooded Surrealist research and its analytical games'. This article contains quite clearly a restatement of the fundamental tenets of *négritude* in relation to Haitian art, but with the constant insistence on the community of cultural and artistic experience of all peoples of Negro origin. The humanism we have seen as part of the concept of *négritude* is Haitian but also common to all peoples of Negro extraction. Negro art appeals to Negroes all over the world. He refers to the 'originality and attraction of aesthetic forms common to countries of Negro origin'.

What does Alexis in fact claim for Haitian art? It is human (no pure art, no ivory towers or intellectual games); it is illogical, but inspired; 'dynamic, it is a living realism' implicating the whole of man, and it is like the art of all other Negro peoples. While there may be much truth in what Alexis claims for Haitian art, the qualities he ascribes to it are not exclusive to the art of Haiti nor to Negro art in general. Would not his qualifications applied to Haitian and Negro art apply equally well to such writers as Pablo Neruda, much of the poetry of F. García Lorca, Paul Eluard, Rafael Alberti, to mention only a few obvious examples of contemporary poets? It is quite clear, I think, that here, and in most of *négritude,* we are faced with an aesthetic mystique and also a racial mystique. Alexis's article, in spite of its apparent objectivity, is basically an emotional statement of an attitude. No doubt the author feels that what he writes is true, as do Césaire and Fanon writing on the same subject.

Much closer to the reality of the situation is Césaire, who, in spite of his early proclamations of *négritude* in an article 'Culture et colonisation' (in the same number of *Présence Africaine*), states: 'One may ask oneself what is the common denominator of an assembly of men [the First International Congress of Black Writers and Poets and Artists] as diverse as Africans from Black Africa and North Americans, West Indians and Malagasies. The answer seems to me obvious; the common denominator is the colonial situation.' And 'all black cultures are developing at the present under a peculiar conditioning which is the colonial, semi-colonial or para-colonial situation'. And the Barbadian, George Lamming, at the same Congress goes even further: 'I think it may be said that politics is the only ground for a universal Negro sympathy.'

While there are obvious objections to Alexis's racial-aesthetic mystique, the purely political interpretation of the interest of Negroes all over the world in each other is not the complete answer either. The political side of *négritude* can be seen clearly in protests against discrimination and economic exploitation. They certainly abound in Caribbean writing and are the concern of the Negro in any part of the world, for the total world situation of the Negro is a quite tangible aspect of *négritude*. The hankering after Africa in the Caribbean, on the other hand, is an indisputable fact, as we shall see in our chapter 'The Theme of Africa', existing at both a popular and an intellectual level. The emotional pull towards Africa as distinct from political sympathy towards Africa is definitely there. It is a compound of historical memories, often of social and economic frustration, and also of the peculiar tension which exists in many West Indians of African origin, who willy-nilly must live in a white man's civilisation, which also through historical circumstances is theirs, or at least the only civilisation they have. Perhaps the acute emotional and somewhat troubled concern of the West Indian with Africa is due to the fact that the West Indian from the predominantly black islands of Haiti, Jamaica, Martinique etc. is placed in an exceptional position to experience the inner tensions and contradictions of a black man forced to live in a world of predominantly white cultural values.

# CHAPTER V

# THE THEME OF AFRICA

IN the 1930s, the theme of Africa became one of the most widely handled by Caribbean poets, particularly in Haiti and the French and British West Indies; not of African civilisations or African cultural values, but of Africa itself as a vague geographical region, and the imaginary and emotional fatherland of all the Negroes in the world. The Caribbean Negro imagines with nostalgia and love an Africa which he rarely knows from direct experience, and his poems about Africa are songs of exile, full of sadness and vague longings. The following poem by Daniel Thaly who, although born in the British island of Dominica writes in French, gives the general feeling of much of this kind of writing:

Do you not hear a distant, plaintive song
Which trails like a pure sobbing in the tropical night?
It could be the sigh of the sea on a reef
At the hour when each wave expires like a dying breath.

The man who is singing in the distance behind the corn
Before the dead ashes of the hearth of his hut
Is an old Congolese who is weeping for his country,
In ecstasy under the light of the moon.

He was no more than a thin, sick young Negro boy
When dressed only in a red loin-cloth,
He crossed the Atlantic on a white slave-ship.

Since then, his soul is haunted with nostalgia;
Nothing has consoled him for the loss of his distant Africa
Where are the blue rivers beloved of the hippopotamus.[1]

Their Caribbean world appears to them full of reminders of Africa—music, dancing, voodoo and the colour of their own skins.

In Haiti in the 1920s writers of the nationalist revival which had been precipitated by the American occupation turned re-

peatedly to the theme. In 1927 the Haitian, Carl Brouard, published his 'Nostalgia', now in almost all anthologies of Haitian
poetry:

> Drum
> when you sound
> my soul screams towards Africa.
> Sometimes
> I dream of an immense jungle
> bathed in moon-light
> with hirsute, sweating figures,
> sometimes
> of a filthy hut
> where I drink blood out of human skulls.[2]

Apart from the feeling of exile, of longing to return 'home', the
poems of Africa take the form of a highly emotional evocation,
through landscapes with imaginary fauna and flora (baobab trees,
jungle, elephants, crocodiles, monkeys), lamentation over past
greatness and present humiliation and also a consciousness of the
'presence' of Africa in the Caribbean people of African origin, of
African customs and words. Under this spell, Caribbean writers
send forth sighs of nostalgia or at times cries of rebellion. The
following prose-poem of Brouard is perhaps one of the best
examples of this trend:

> Your lost sons send you greetings, Mother Africa. From the West Indies
> to Bermuda, and from Bermuda to the United States, they sigh after you,
> they dream of your baobab-trees and of the blue gum-trees full of tucans.
> In the night of their dream, Timbuktu is a mysterious onyx, a black diamond.
> The warriors have departed for the land of the dead. The empire of Mandingo
> has fallen like a dry leaf. Is there any part of the world where they do not tell
> the rosary of their misfortunes? The children pay for the sins of the fathers
> to the fourth generation, you said, Lord. But the curse of Ham still lasts.

> How long, Oh Lord?
> Consolation for the afflicted, elixir for those who suffer, water for the
> thirsty; dream, mysterious Negro drum, lull the nostalgic Hamites, put to
> sleep their immemorial anguish.[3]

Other typical examples are 'Racial Drum', by Maurice
Casséus:

> Let us hear, oh, conical racial drum
> your great African rhythm, your nocturnal voice.

and let me embrace to my soul that savage song
which you dedicate to the murdered land,
which in myself, secretly I adore.[4]

And Paul Laraque's 'Transplanted':

Heavy with all the languor brought back from the country
The anguish of the ju-ju men bathing my eyes,
I have felt on nights of African restlessness
I have felt the soul of the world hostile to my race.[5]

Poems similar in style and content abound in Haitian literature. Their most constant common features are an emotional identification with Africans as racial brothers and an atavistic feeling for the land of Africa. Africa appears as a sort of lost paradise, a Negro Arcadia, before the arrival of the Europeans and the 'moment of the uprooting' by the slave-traders. It is a place where the displaced Negro has his roots and where he lived freely his own way of life. And as we have seen, Africa is used by many writers to reject Europe, which had humiliated and repudiated the Negro.

This passion for Africa, so common in Haitian literature, was, however, not without its critics who felt that such an attitude was wrong and out of place as far as Haiti was concerned. Some felt it was an insincere pose. Sténio Vincent writes ironically of Africanising Haitian intellectuals:

Paris was their headquarters. Which one of them would have dreamed of actually going to some part of the Sudan or the Congo to enter into communion with the souls of our distant Mandingo or Bantu ancestors? Do you know any one of them who has made this pilgrimage? I do not. I do know that they prefer the Boulevard des Italiens to the swamps of Bahr-el-Ghazal or the mountains of Kilimanjaro.[6]

From Dantès Bellegarde comes a fundamental criticism which implies a totally different concept of the nature of Haitian culture. In fact, Bellegarde, of the same generation as the leader of the Africanising school, Jean Price-Mars, makes an apologia for Haiti as a cultural province of France. 'We belong to Africa by our blood', he writes, 'and to France by our spirit and by a significant proportion of our blood.'[7] And he continues to flay the Africanisers, pointing out what he considers to be the paradox of their behaviour as intellectuals—on the one hand Africanising primitivism and on the other French-style hyper-intellectualism:

Some Haitians, who want a closed and self-sufficient Haiti, have taken offence because I observed that Haiti is an intellectual province of France, just as it offends them that the Catholic Church of Haiti is an ecclesiastical province of the Church of Rome. They don't want to hear about French or even Latin culture. What is good enough for Walloon Belgium, for French Switzerland or French Canada, is not good enough for Haiti. It should therefore set itself the ideal of becoming in the middle of America a small Dahomeyan island, with a Bantu culture and a Congolese religion to entertain Yankee tourists and please the Seabrooks and the Loederers, who are on the look out for the sensational. This does not prevent our aesthetes from proclaiming themselves Baudelairians, Proustians, Futurists or Surrealists.[8]

It is true that some of the cult of Africa reached the Haitian intellectuals of the 1920s and 1930s through French influence since, as we have seen, African primitivism was fashionable in European intellectual circles. The Negro renaissance in the United States[9] was undoubtedly another influence, as was the general ideological climate of Europe and the United States, impregnated with aggressive nationalism and racialism. However, it would be a mistake to attribute their feeling for Africa exclusively to extraneous sources and not to take into account their genuine, emotional attraction to Africa. It existed at a practical level in the campaigning by the Jamaican, Marcus Garvey, for the return of all Negroes to Africa, a plan which Garvey worked hard to implement. The response to Garvey's project was the measure of the sincerity of this deep-rooted popular feeling. It also exists at the popular level in the Rastafarian sect of Jamaica, from the confusion of whose ideas one thing emerges clearly: they want to go back to Africa. For them Africa is the Promised Land of all Negroes. In Haiti, too, although there has never been any movement comparable to Garvey's 'back to Africa' movement, the African tradition is strong among the people. Voodoo and a great deal of its terminology is of clear African origin, as well as many popular customs. Africa ('Guinée') lives in many proverbs and folk sayings, and let us not forget the old belief among the slaves that the soul of the slave returns to Africa when he dies.[10] This tradition has been taken up by Jacques Roumain in one of his most effective poems, 'The Slow Road to Guinea':

> It's the slow road to Guinea
> Death takes you down

Here are the boughs, the trees, the forest
Listen to the sound of the wind in its long hair
  of eternal night

It's the slow road to Guinea
Where your fathers await you without impatience
Along the way, they talk
They wait
This is the hour when the streams rattle
  like beads of bone

It's the slow road to Guinea
No bright welcome will be made for you
In the dark land of dark men:
Under a smoky sky pierced by the cry of birds
Around the eye of the river
        the eyelashes of the trees open on decaying light
There, there awaits you beside the water a quiet village
And the hut of your fathers, and the hard ancestral stone
        where your head will rest at last.[11]

This dream of Africa is very often blended with the lamentation over Africa's past greatness and present humiliation. The following poem of Claude McKay is very typical of this kind of lament over the ruin of Africa—the Pharaohs, the pyramids, the Sphinx, the ancient cultures of central Africa—such are the most common features of these poems.

The sun sought thy dim bed and brought out light.
The sciences were sucklings at thy breasts;
When all the world was young in pregnant night,
The slaves toiled at the monumental best.
Thou ancient treasure house, thou modern prize,
New peoples marvel at thy pyramids.
The years roll on, thy sphinx of riddle eyes
Watches the mad world with immobile lids.
The Hebrews humbled them at Pharaoh's name.
Cradle of power. Yet all things were in vain,
Honour and glory, arrogance and fame.
They went. The darkness swallowed thee again,
Thou art the harlot, now thy time is done,
Of all the mighty nations of the sun.[12]

However, not all is sadness, dreamy nostalgia and lamentation over the past glories of Africa in Caribbean writing on this theme.

The Jamaican poet, George Campbell, makes a fusion of the robust peasant women of Jamaica and his idea of Africa; she is both Jamaican and African and the tone is one of optimism and hope in the African (and Jamaican) future:

> She sings of the African womb
> Everlasting above the tomb
> She sings of her island Jamaica
> She sings of the glory of Africa.[13]

And the tone of Aimé Césaire's poem 'To Greet the Third World' is one of jubilation at the awakening of black Africa, a greeting from the 'distant isle' to the newly independent African states:

> I see Africa, multiple and one
> vertical in the tumultuous events
> with its swellings and nodules
> rather apart, but within reach
> of the century, like a heart in reserve.
>
> And I say again: Hoo mother
>     and I raise my strength
>     bending down my face.
>     Oh, my land
> Let me break it gently between my thumb
>                     and my fore-finger
> Let me rub my chest, my arms
> my left arm
> Let me caress my right arm with it.
>
> Hoo, my land is good
>     your voice also is good
>     with that peace
>     that the sun-set brings.
>
>         .     .     .     .     .
>
> Look:
>
> Africa is no longer
> in the diamond of misfortune
> a black heart splitting[14]

One of the most complete pieces of fantasy writing about Africa is *The Leopard* (1958) by the Jamaican, Vic Reid. It is set in Kenya during the Mau Mau revolt, and involves the killing of a white man by an African ('half Kikuyu, half Masai'), and the subsequent hunting of the African by a leopard. Whatever the symbolic or allegorical significance of the novel, Reid has tried to pour himself into a completely African character. The background too, naturally, is African.

The theme of Africa hardly exists in the literature of Cuba, Puerto Rico or the Dominican Republic. The fact that the Negro population of these three islands is smaller than that of Jamaica, Trinidad, Haiti etc., however, does not seem to be a sufficient explanation. What seems more likely is that there is a lack of awareness of Africa in the Spanish-speaking islands, due to an almost total lack of contact. British and French West Indians meet and mix with Africans in London and Paris and the same applies to Haitians, many of whom study in France. And as well as these contacts as colonies, the British and French territories had a feeling of solidarity and sympathy with the peoples of other colonial territories, strengthened by the fact that they are of the same race. Culturally, Cuba and the Dominican Republic are more drawn towards Latin America, and to a lesser degree towards Spain, where African contacts and concern for Africa are slight. In the United States the many Puerto Rican inhabitants appear to feel very little identification with American Negroes, and much less with Africans.

Apart from occasional references to Africa in the Afro-Cuban writers there is only one writer of the Spanish Caribbean who shows a marked interest in Africa. This is the Puerto Rican Luis Palés Matos, who in his book *Tun tun de pasa y grifería* has a number of poems with an African setting. Basically they are Afro-Cuban in spirit and style—full of sensuality, primitivism and rhythmical nonsense words. But Palés Matos has gone a step further. He feels the presence of Africa in the Afro-Caribbean setting, so imports into his poetry what he feels are typical African elements—African animals: hippopatami, gorillas, crocodiles, and a more fundamental form of voodoo, involving cannibalism. In one poem in particular the significance of Africa to Palés Matos is very clear. This is the poem 'Numen', which presents the basic Afro-Caribbean primitiveness, the animality of the Negro which come to him from the land of his ancestors. In the possession of the dance, the Negro returns to his basic African primitiveness:

African jungle—Tembandumba.
Haitian bush—Macandal.
It is Negro land. The Negro dances.
The Negro dances in solitude.
Travelling immense distances.
Over the dance his soul flies
To the dark limbo where rules
The essential Negro formula.
The hippopotamus gives him his strength.
The crocodile gives him its armour.
The snake gives him its stealth.
The antelope agility.
And the powerful elephant,
Crushing jungles as it passes,
Opens the way towards the deep
and eternal ancestral spirit.[15]

Palés Matos saw in this primitivism a release from the tensions
of Western intellectualism and a vital creative force in the arts.
In this, of course, he was merely participating in the general
orientation of the Afro-Cuban movement, in the fashionable
cult of the primitive.

Many of his fellow Puerto Ricans were upset by his insistence
on the African substratum of feeling in Puerto Rico and were
clearly irritated by his constant bringing of Africa into a Puerto
Rican setting. Tomás Blanco wrote: 'The incarnation of an interpretation of the Negro race in all its purity is an exotic element
in Puerto Rico. It corresponds rather to a characteristic tendency
of the contemporary spirit [Afro-Cubanism] to exalt vital forces
. . .'[16] Another Puerto Rican, Margot Arce, on the other hand,
accepts Matos's Africanism as something genuinely Puerto Rican:

Puerto Rican, we all know, are his Negro woman who sings of her sober
domestic life and the Negro boy who answers with a: 'Yes, master.' Puerto
Rican is the background landscape of these poems. Puerto Rican are the
sensibility and the way it is expressed and Puerto Rican is the spiritual atmosphere which is born from the pressing rhythms, the sensual and colourful
images, the smooth, sweet language.[17]

Apart from certain exaggerations, it would appear true that
these 'Africanising' poems of Palés Matos have captured an
aspect of Caribbean life, have caught something in the general
atmosphere of all the Caribbean countries. To point out that

there are very few pure Negroes in Puerto Rico is beside the point. The Negro has left a deep imprint on the Caribbean way of life, not only in music, dancing, customs, food, religious beliefs and practices, language—all things which are easily verifiable as of African origin—but in something more subtle in the spirit of the place, not so much a way of life as a feeling of life.

Palés Matos is an isolated example of Spanish-Caribbean concern with Africa, whether real or imagined. On the other hand, Africa as an object of dreams and fantasies is very common in the literature of the British and French West Indies, an ever-recurring obsession. It may be that with the emergence of the new African states and a more frequent cultural interchange with the *real* Africa, this theme of Africa as a country of the heart will disappear. In the meantime it has, over a number of years, produced poems possessing a curiously haunting quality of exile and nostalgia.

# CHAPTER VI

# REVOLT

WE have already seen attacks levelled against Western civilisation's treatment of the Negro in the past (the ransacking of Africa for slaves, the slave-trade, the brutalities of slavery in the Caribbean), and we have seen the rejection of Western cultural values balanced by an affirmation of African or Negro counter-values. The present chapter deals with a more limited aspect of what is perhaps fundamentally the same or a closely associated attitude, namely the idea of the revolt which will put an end to the subjugation and inferior status of the Negro, revolt often envisaged in terms of destruction and revenge. The expression of this feeling is found largely in poetry, which is perhaps not surprising, as it is highly emotional and in many cases very personal. We have already seen the romantic slave in Avellaneda's *Sab* indulging in dreams of bloodshed and ruin, and this attitude of impassioned individual revolt accompanied by the punishing of the white man for all his crimes against the Negro race ('the crime against God, the crime against man, the crime of *lèse-Afrique*' as the Guadeloupean writer Paul Niger puts it[1]) is a common one in the poets of the first fifty years of the twentieth century.

It is in Haiti that the theme is found in greatest abundance. Although we have mentioned it before, we cannot stress too much the importance of the war of independence which the Haitian Negroes waged and won. This struggle has come subsequently to be regarded by Haitians as a crusade on behalf of the whole Negro race. The memory of the victory over the French is kept alive as *the* great national historical memory of the Haitian people and serves as a permanent source of national pride. Haitian literature throughout the nineteenth century abounds in works dealing with episodes in the war often centering around the figures of the Haitian leaders—heroes such as Dessalines, Toussaint L'Ouverture, Henri Christophe, Ogé etc. The general tone of much of this literature is well and characteristically given

in Oswald Durand's poem 'The Epic of our Forefathers', composed for the first centenary of Haitian independence in 1904:

> Hark, hark, it is another Iliad,
> It has its black Achilles and its Agamemnon.
> Each name was engraved on our hearts with iron.
> They are living dead. A whole Pleiad.[2]

Bearing in mind the intense pride of the Haitians in their
independence and status as the first black republic, it is easy to
understand their feelings when in 1916 the island was occupied
by the United States, an occupation which lasted until 1934.
Haitian intellectuals reacted by an intensification of national
feeling and, as we have seen, by drawing towards their African
roots. In 1931 Jean Brierre published *Tomorrow's Flag* in
which he compares the situation under American occupation
with that on the eve of the revolt against the French at the end of
the eighteenth century. Needless to say, the tone of the poem is
angry and violent:

> Let all the proud mountain tops of the island come together
> And together send forth a single roar,
> Which will bring down the filthy servitude,
> For blood is needed to inscribe the rights of the Negro.
> Our people hides under its peaceful appearance
> The fury of the avenger and the soul of heroes.[3]

In another poem, 'Black', by the Haitian Regnor C. Bernard,
the theme of revolt and revenge for the humiliations suffered by
the Negro is clearly stated:

> An immense fire which my continuous suffering
> and your sneers
> and your inhumanity
> and your scorn
> and your disdain
> have lighted in the depths of my heart
> will swallow you all.[4]

And the French Guianian, Léon Damas, in a poem entitled
'They Have', threatens the white world with a great racial up-
heaval which he sees as imminent:

> They have fixed things so well
> fixed things so well

that one day everything
we kicked everything in the air
kicked everything in the air ourselves.
And yet, it would not take much
not much at all
for everything to go in one day
to go
to go our way
the way of our race
ours ours
It would not take much.[5]

And again, the Haitian Jacques Roumain in his revolutionary 'Ebony', already quoted in part, an anti-clerical poem, full of crudities and written in coarse popular French, threatens punishment and humiliations for the agents of the Church which, like so many extreme left-wing Caribbean intellectuals, he sees as an instrument for keeping the Negro in his place:

Surprise
Jesus Mary Joseph
when we catch the missionary by the beard
laughing horribly
to teach him in our turn
by kicking his bottom
that our ancestors were not Gauls,
and that we don't give a damn
for a God who,
if he is the father,
well, we, the dirty niggers,
it is obvious that we must be his bastard sons,
and it won't help yelling
Jesus Mary Joseph
like an old bladder spilling over with lies
we must once and for all
teach you to preach confiteors with a whip
humility
resignation
to our miserable lot
of Negroes, of niggers, of dirty niggers.[6]

It is quite apparent that the poems quoted are the outcome of intense personal emotion. Roumain's poem splutters out a furious invective, only capable of expression in argot crudities.

Damas's poem also appears to have been written in a paroxysm of intense emotion and we are by no means surprised to find an ideological statement of the principle of Negro revolt in his introduction to *Poets Writing in French (1900–1945)*:

The wind which is rising from black America will soon have cleansed our Caribbean of the aborted fruits of a decaying culture. Langston Hughes and Claude McKay, both poets of revolution, have brought us, preserved in red alcohol, African love of life, African joy of love and the African dream of death.[7]

Yet it is in McKay that we find the most poignant expression of the Negro revolt against persecution and humiliation in his well-known poem:

If we must die, let it not be like hogs
Hunted and penned in an inglorious spot,
While round us bark the mad and hungry dogs,
Making their mock of our accursed lot.
If we must die, O let us nobly die

.     .     .     .     .

And for their thousand blows deal one death blow.
What though before us lies the open grave?
Like men we'll face the murderous cowardly pack
Pressed to the wall, dying, but fighting back.[8]

Although McKay in this poem makes no direct mention of the Negro and his situation, it is safe to assume that he had them in mind and that they were indeed the source of inspiration of the poem, taking into account the tone and general orientation of his work. Nevertheless, the poem transcends the immediate situation of the Negro and stands as an impassioned cry of defiance in the name of any persecuted people who have their backs to the wall.

In the Cuban *Revista de Avance* (February 1930), at the height of the Afro-Cuban fashion, appeared the story 'Lucumí Dance' by Luis Felipe Rodríguez, about an old Negro who has been a cane-cutter all his life and who remembers in his bouts of drunkenness how he and his father were brought from Africa and were dumped on the shores of Cuba 'like sacks of dried meat'. In one of these fits of blind drunkenness his long-contained hatred against the sugar-estate bursts forth and he sets fire to the cane-field and dances while it burns, singing: 'I am going to punish you, cane-field, the old Negro is going to punish you.' It is quite clear that the cane-field symbolises for this simple man the system under which he and other Negroes have been made to suffer and slave.[9] It is possible that the story is partly inspired by 'The Black Tsar' by Paul Morand which appeared in an earlier number of the *Revista de Avance* (January 1929), a short story in which a Haitian Negro blows up an American club in Port-au-Prince where Negroes were not admitted.

In other writers, however, the nature of the Negro revolt is seen in clearer and much less personal terms, seen in fact as part of a great world-wide proletarian uprising. We have seen in our chapter on *négritude* that Roumain and Césaire, both Marxists at the time of writing the poems in question, had to remind themselves that in their denunciations of the white world they meant white *bourgeois*, the white capitalist world, and that the oppressed and exploited Negro of South Africa or certain parts of the United States was at one with white workers suffering under the same system.

In his 'Tomorrow's Flag', Jean Brierre makes vague threats about the Negro's revenge, but in 'Black Soul' he has a much more clearly defined attitude. After enumerating the Negro's participation in history and his humiliation, he writes:

> You are waiting for the call which will soon come,
> for the inevitable mobilisation,
> for your war has only had a succession of truces.[10]

And Jacques Roumain in 'Ebony':

> it will be too late, I tell you,
> For even the tomtoms have learned the language
> of the Internationale.
> All together
> the dirty Indians
> the dirty Indo-Chinese
> the dirty Arabs
> the dirty Malayans
> the dirty Jews
> the dirty landowners
> and we are all on our feet
> all the damned ones of the earth.[11]

And the same poet in 'The New Negro Sermon ':

> No brothers, comrades,
> We shall pray no more
> Our revolt rises like the cry of a stormbird over the rotten
> splashing of the marshes
> We shall no longer sing our sad despairing spirituals
> Another song shall surge from our throats
> We unfurl our red flags
> Stained with the blood of our heroes
> Under this sign we shall march
> Under this sign we march
> Up the damned of the earth
> Up the prisoners of hunger.[12]

(The first lines of the *Internationale* in French.)

It appears then that the feeling of revolt, the deep emotional urge to destroy the white world and to punish the white man follows two lines, one of individual, probably anarchistic anger (Bernard, Damas, the early Brierre, Rodríguez) and the other a Marxist or Communist line in which the Negro's revolt is part of the world-wide uprising of the underprivileged and the oppressed. However, perhaps the most remarkable thing about the Negro-Marxist writing is that the strain of racial resentment is so strong that at times it almost overshadows the appeal to the workers of the world. Damas's poems in *Pigments*, so often quoted in this book, are described by Robert Desnos in the Introduction as: 'a gift from the savannah to the factory, from the plantation to the farm, from the tropical factory to the work-shop'. He also describes them as being dedicated to the 'immense proletariat of the colonies', yet the general tenor of these poems is of violent racial hatred—hatred of everything white. The same applies to much of the writing of Jacques Roumain and Aimé Césaire, both nevertheless declared and active Communists. We have observed that in order to break the prestige of Western culture it was necessary to discredit it, very often by attitudes of deliberate disrespect ranging from scornful criticism to abusive vitupera-tion. This was apparently felt to be a necessary stage in the breaking of its stranglehold on the Negro; perhaps in the calls to revolt and the threats of violent revenge it was felt by Marxist writers that capitalism should be embodied in the white man and in the white man's way of life and that the most effective means of rousing the black proletariat against the capitalist system was to make the white man the target of their calls to action.

# CHAPTER VII

# THE COLOURED WOMAN IN CARIBBEAN POETRY

IN an angry, resentful book, *The Cuban Negro*, Antonio Arredondo refers to what he calls the 'sexual tragedy of the Negro'
and derives it from the imposition through white culture of a
particular concept of human beauty, especially of feminine
beauty, which he generalises as made up of 'pink and white face,
green eyes, a skin of alabaster and golden hair'.[1] Expanding on
the subject he writes:

> The best canvases by the most famous painters display virgins and madon-
> nas who are never black or mulatto. The verses of the most famous poets are
> written to praise the charms of white women. In the theatre the heroines are
> white actresses. Even the Cuban mulatto poet Plácido writes of white women.
> In beauty competitions, the aesthetic canons are based on white women.
> Heroines in films are always white. And as for the poor coloured girl, her
> heroes are always a Clark Gable, a Valentino or a Robert Taylor. She has
> never read a novel in which a man of black skin, thick lips and woolly hair is
> anything but a butler, boot-black or servant.[2]

All this forms part of what he calls 'the Negro's disdain of the
Negro'. Now while in a general way this is true, particularly as
far as popular culture (films, detective novels, etc.) is concerned,
if one looks into the literature of those Caribbean countries where
a more or less great proportion of the population is coloured, it
becomes abundantly clear that not only is the coloured woman,
black or mulatto, presented in a favourable aesthetic light, but
the subject of her beauty is so frequent as to be a commonplace
throughout the literature of the whole area. The theme, however,
appears with several variants in the course of its development,
and it will be the object of this chapter to trace and analyse these
variants in Caribbean literature written in Spanish, French and
English.

It is in the literature of Haiti that we find the first deliberate and self-conscious evaluation of the beauty of the black woman. Haiti had emerged, full of national pride, from its war of independence against France—which was at that time (1804) the greatest military power in the world—and in the course of the nineteenth century Haitian writers devoted themselves to strengthening the foundations of national feeling by referring continually to the heroic efforts of the black slaves who had obtained such an amazing victory. There is in their work an intense and, often, defensive love for everything Haitian, and among subjects to which they directed their literary efforts was the Haitian woman who was, of course, black and of negroid features. As early as 1868 we find a poem by Pierre Faubert entitled 'The Negress':

> I am proud to tell you, oh Negress, that I love you
> and that your black colour pleases me. Do you know why?
> It is because noble virtues, chaste heart, even beauty,
> everything that delights me, has been given you by heaven.
>
> Innocent victim of an absurd prejudice,
> look at yourself in the water in the light of dawn,
> and see how your eyes are fair with a supreme gift,
> source of devotion, and which we name love.[3]

In another poem, 'Our Country Girls' (1898), Oswald Durand celebrates the sensual beauty of the black or mulatto girl in the following terms:

> If one day my muse asks me
> for some verses—an ode, a sonnet,
> I shall offer her the most subtle couplet.
> I shall not go, leaving the New World,
> to tune my lute for the white and blue-eyed maiden,
> neither for the brunette, nor the red-head or the blonde,
> pale beneath their misty skies,
> but I shall sing to my black girl,
> whose mad caress
> intoxicates my heart,
> I shall offer her verses and songs.
> I shall sing of her lip
> which never tires,
> and which kindles in me passion
> and its charming torments . . .[4]

In both these poems there is, however, a clear awareness of doing something new and unusual. Both poets knew they were going against a European literary tradition by singing the praises of black female beauty. In this poem and others ('Idalina' and the well-known 'Choucoune', written in Creole), Durand celebrates the beauty of black women with the emphasis on their sensuality, the voluptuousness of their figures and with a certain element which I have called fruit imagery, the tendency to compare various features of the black or mulatto woman with character-istic fruits of the tropics. It is well known that in the nineteenth century one of the devices most common in American literature to lend it a distinctive tonality, was the use of local names and names of fruits, trees and flowers—very often of Amerindian origin. This tendency seems to have fused with the praise of the beauty of women of African extraction. In Oswald Durand (1840–1906) we find the comparison of 'hair' with 'rice-field', 'breasts' with 'sapodillas', 'lips' with 'star-apples'. This equation, the coloured woman–fruit imagery, seems to have established itself spontaneously. We find it again in Dominique Hyppolyte's 'Loetitia—La Noire':

> Under the green branches of the avocado tree
> let us go and savour love like a fine fruit . . .[5]

The equation reaches its climax, almost a *reductio ad absur-dum*, in the well-known poem of the Haitian, Émile Roumer, which begins:

> High-yellow of my heart, with breasts like tangerines,
> you taste better to me than eggplant stuffed with crab,
> you are the tripe in my pepper-pot,
> the dumpling in my peas, my tea of aromatic herbs.
> You are the corned beef whose customhouse is my heart,
> my mush with syrup that trickles down the throat.
> You are a steaming dish, mushroom cooked with rice,
> crisp potato fries, and little fish fried brown . . .[6]

The tendency to comparisons with fruits appears to spring from two sources. In the first place it is traditional for European lyricism to seek comparisons between the physical attributes of women and flowers (lily, rose, carnation etc.). The Caribbean poet has simply substituted for these traditional elements the names of local flowers and of local fruits. It would seem, however, that there is a significant change of emphasis in the attitude to the woman, for while flowers are appreciated for their beauty of shape and colour and in some cases their perfume, fruits and vegetables (and we have seen that the Haitians do not hesitate to use vegetal comparisons) are eaten. So that the use of fruit analogies would seem to reflect a different attitude—an attitude of frank sensuality which, as is clear from the literary production of the Caribbean, is perhaps the predominant note in the West Indian attitude to life. Secondly, the praise of the beauty of the coloured woman in Caribbean literature also appears to be closely linked with the general current of literary Americanism, which flows from the early beginnings of cultural independence in Latin America, and which is far from exhausted even today. As the predominant feature in literary Americanism is precisely the description of nature in America, it is not surprising that there should have been a fusion of local colour and the local woman.

So we have the equation of woman (homeland and its products) with sensuality and fertility. The combination of these elements is clearly seen in a very remarkable poem by the Puerto Rican poet Luis Palés Matos, in which he makes his 'mulata' a symbol of what is most vital and characteristic of Caribbean life, land, climate, rhythm, music, sensuality and racial vitality:

> Now you are, mulatto girl,
> the whole sea and land of my island.
> Fruital symphony whose scales
> burst out furiously in the smell of your body.
> Here is the sapodilla in its green suit,
> with its fine and soft muslin pants, here is the star-apple
> with its childish milk; here the pineapple
> with its soprano's crown. All the fruits, oh mulatto girl,
> you offer me all the fruits in the clear bay of your body,
> burnished by the suns of the tropics.[7]

But apart from the purely literary aspects of this theme there is no doubt that writers, particularly in Haiti and the French and British West Indies, are seeking a new aesthetic orientation in the sense of a revaluation of beauty favourable to the Negro. We have seen how Faubert and Durand bring into their poems in praise of coloured women a mixture of reticence and challenge. Even in a poem like Philippe Thoby Marcellin's 'Petite noire' (1926) there is a challenging note:

Thick lips, flat nose, she is really ugly, the little black girl,
really ugly,
and very black, like all the sins. But you smile
and it is a festival of angels.
Sweetness of your white eyes,
purity of your white teeth,
I shall sing of you, little black girl, it is your turn now.
I shall speak of the grace of your body, straight as a palm-tree,
but supple as a flame.
I shall speak of your rhythmical walk, when walking in a line,
perfumed with balm and mint, you bring down from the hills
the fruits and vegetables of Kenscoff and Furcy.[8]

In the Jamaican, George Campbell, there is a more serious
tone as he sings of the beauty and fertility of the Negro woman,
linking his praise with the biblical tradition in the Song of Solo-
mon:

> Oh Solomon's fair
> Oh shadowed flower.
>
> Not black
> blue sky in face.
>
> Oh woven of the night
> this beauty of her race.
>
> Oh glorious peak
> procreative power
> the woman Eve
> twixt dark and light
> Oh Solomon's fair
> Oh shadowed flower.[9]

The Puerto Rican poet Luis Llorens Torres also resorts to the
biblical reference, 'Nigra sum, sed formosa' in his poem 'Negra',
which also contains the ever-present fruit analogies: the complexion has the 'colour of Morocco leather'; the teeth are compared to the 'foam of coconut milk' and the thighs to 'maho-
gany'.[10]

Another aspect of the rehabilitation of the Negro woman in
Caribbean literature is a criticism of the white woman as being
over-civilised, over-sophisticated. In contrast the Negro woman
appears more elemental, more of a woman. Lionel Attuly, a
Martinican, writes in scornful terms of white women and, by
implication, of white civilisation:

And she talked and talked and talked.
Outside it was snowing and cold.
It is a pity they cannot bring you that too,
along with the rest of their civilisation.
With the brassières and corsets,
the garters and the girdles,
and smugness,
and ignorance,
and the lie of alliances,
and words
and all the rest of it.

and take from you in exchange
your bodies of supple hard metal,
the dignity of your silence,
in the gift of pleasure
your sacred wombs the hope of all humanity.

I have refound my place in the hollow of your shoulder
on your breast a real breast,
capable of supporting the weight of a man's head
of slaking the thirst for peace in a man's heart
for feeding a man's hunger for pleasure
without betrayal.[11]

This kind of aggressiveness is part of a broader attitude to be found in many Caribbean Negro intellectuals, a critical rejection of European or 'white' cultural values. Another poet, the French Guianian, Léon Damas, expresses in *Pigments* the same kind of repugnance for white women (and white civilisation) in bitter and rancorous accents:

Give me back my black dolls
let them dispel
the image of the pale mercenary vendors of love
who come and go
along the boulevard of my boredom.

Give me back my black dolls so I can play with them
the naïve games of my instinct
remain in the shadow of its laws
recover my courage
my daring
feel myself again

> a new self which I was yesterday
> without complexities yesterday
> at the time of the up-rooting.[12]

The Jamaican poet, Adolphe Roberts, in 'Maroon Girl', after filling in a back-cloth of typical Jamaican scenery, makes his Maroon girl a symbol of the strength and pride of Jamaica:

> She is a peasant, yet she is a queen.
> She is Jamaica poised against attack.
> Her woods are hung with orchids; the still flame
> of red hibiscus lights her path, and starred
> with orange and coffee blossoms is her yard.
> She stands on the ground for which her fathers died;
> Figure of savage beauty, figure of pride.[13]

So far, we have seen the rehabilitation of the coloured woman in Caribbean literature manifesting itself in the praise of her beauty, her sensuality and capacity for physical love. These poems tend towards the sensual and physical and at the same time are often linked with the exaltation of the writers' native lands with all that is most typical in their flora. Another factor in the aesthetic rehabilitation of the coloured woman is the general trend towards revaluation of Negro art and the Negro idea of beauty linked with the Negro renaissance of the 1920s. In the Caribbean it was the Jamaican, Marcus Garvey, who gave the fullest expression to this trend in his revaluation of the total situation of the Negro in the world. In his attempt to restore to Negroes a sense of pride in their own race, and as an enemy of miscegenation, he did not forget the Negro woman—considered 'ugly' by European standards and indeed rejected in favour of white or light-coloured women by many Negroes who had accepted white standards of feminine beauty. In one of his very bad, but very forceful, poems he eulogises the black Venus in enthusiastic, emphatic terms:

> Black queen of beauty, thou hast given colour to the world.
> Among other women thou art royal and fairest.
> Like the brightest jewel in the regal diadem,
> Shin'st thou, Goddess of Africa, Nature's purest emblem.
> Black men worship at thy virginal shrine of purest love,
> Because in thine eyes are virtue's steady and holy mark,
> As we see no other, clothed in silk or fine linen,
> From ancient Venus, the Goddess, to mythical Helen.[14]

In order to break the hold of the white standard of beauty, Garvey recommended black mothers to give their children black dolls, and the Bishop of the African Orthodox Church which was founded by Garvey in 1924, advised Negroes to burn pictures of the white Virgin and Child if they happened to have them in their houses. At the Fourth Convention of Negro Peoples, held in New York in 1924, the priests of Garvey's church marched under an enormous portrait of a black Virgin.

Another variant of the theme of the coloured woman is to be found in the 'Afro-Cuban' movement of the period 1920–40. Afro-Cubanism was a conscious attempt to be primitive, and in spite of its Cuban or Caribbean setting was a reflection of the European fashion of the 1920s for the primitive, although, as Ramón Guirao put it, 'vitalised by contact with the human document'. The Negro figures, male or female, invariably appear in an atmosphere of violence, heavy sensuality, frenetic dancing and drumming and voodooesque possession. In the case of the female dancer, the most animal and sensuous aspects of her appearance and movements are emphasised, as in Luis Palés Matos' well-known 'Negro Town', where his black girl smells of 'earth, game and sex' as she sings of her 'sober life of a domestic animal'. So with their deliberate accent on primitivism, the Afro-Cuban writers presented the coloured woman as distorted, disfigured, as a grotesque. Even in Nicolás Guillén (the only coloured poet of the movement and the most outstanding), whose poetry assumed tones of protest and indignation at racial discrimination, we find the same sensual, fiery rumba-dancers, the accent on their primitivism, their animality, as in his 'Madrigal':

> Your belly knows more than your head,
> and as much as your thighs,
> it is strong black grace
> in your naked body.
>
> Your body worthy of the jungle,
> with its red necklaces,
> its bracelets of curving gold,
> and that black alligator
> swimming in the Zambezi of your eyes.[15]

It is interesting to note that neither Haiti nor the British and

French West Indies have produced anything comparable to Afro-Cubanism. To the writers of these countries the Negro was more than a grotesque dancing figure, and when they paint the woman of their race, although they tend to stress her sensuality they do not make her into a caricature, reducing her to the level of a sexual animal without thought or feeling. In sharp contrast to the Afro-Cuban attitude, although the *mise en scène* is the same—a black girl dancing in a cabaret—is a poem by the Jamaican writer, Claude McKay:

> Applauding youths laughed with the young prostitute
> And watched her perfect, half-clad body sway,
> Her voice was like the sound of blended flutes
> Blown by black players on a picnic day,
> She sang and danced on gracefully and calm,
> The light gauze hanging loose about her form;
> To me she seemed a proudly swaying palm,
> Grown lovelier from passing through the storm
> Upon her swarthy neck the black curls
> Luxuriant fell; and tossing coins in praise
> The wine-flushed, bold-eyed boys, and even the girls
> Devoured her shape with eager, passionate gaze;
> But looking at her falsely smiling face,
> I knew that she was not in that strange place.[16]

And in the tender and moving poem 'Nedjé' by the Haitian, Roussan Camille, the feelings inspired in him by the black dancing girl in a cabaret in Casablanca go far beyond her sensual form and feline grace of movement. He sees in her the degradation of a race and also a hope for the future of that race:

> Your slim arms
> raised among the smoke
> yearned to embrace
> centuries of pride
> and miles of landscape
> while your feet
> on the waxed mosaic floor
> searched for the roughness
> of the roads you had trodden in your childhood.[17]

The poets of Haiti, Jamaica and the French West Indies, when they speak of the coloured woman, exalt her beauty and fertility, but not as a literary game or as a picturesque, regionalist theme.

They do so with their spirits charged with love for their race, and with the aim of underlining a type of beauty which until very recently had been considered ugliness. One of the fundamental trends in the Caribbean over the last fifty years has been the revaluation of all aspects of Negro life, in both the past and present. The affirmation of the beauty of the coloured woman (and man) is only a part of this movement which embraces everything from politics to aesthetics.[18]

# CHAPTER VIII

# SOCIAL AND PSYCHOLOGICAL
# PROBLEMS

THE object of this chapter is to deal with works in which questions of race and colour intervene in social and psychological behaviour and attitudes, and in which the situation of the individual, whether as writer or character in a story or novel, and his relationship with the society in which he lives, are determined or affected by these factors.

Let us first examine briefly the circumstances in the Caribbean which give rise to these problems, for they are problems about which writers feel strongly, indeed at times violently. In the first place, no Caribbean country has any discriminative legislation against coloured people such as exists in some parts of the United States and in the Union of South Africa. Since the abolition of slavery, the coloured man has been legally free and equal. But until comparatively recently, within the last twenty years or so, there has in fact been a tendency to prefer white or light-skinned people in the Civil Service, in commerce and in public places such as hotels and shops. This kind of discrimination has varied from island to island. In the British and French Caribbean shade has played little part in government employment since 1945. In Cuba and the Dominican Republic, however, men of dark complexion are rare in the higher ranges of government, indeed so rare that the few that *do* hold such posts are conspicuous. This continues to be true of the Dominican Republic, but in Cuba since the advent of Fidel Castro's regime there has been a positive attempt to bring coloured Cubans into more important public positions. Again, until quite recently, certain hotels and clubs were exclusive and either discouraged or refused admission to coloured people, with the exception of a few very rich ones. This was true of the British and French West Indies, of the Dominican Republic and of Cuba, and while this situation can be said to exist no longer (in Cuba, again, only since the advent of Castro) it is still remembered and rankles with many people who well remember the old days. In Cuba, the Dominican Republic and Puerto Rico, the rich, well-established families were in the past completely exclusive from a colour point of view, and in the British and French islands there were, and still are, certain families who regard themselves as white and adopt an exclusive extremely snobbish attitude towards their coloured compatriots. In commerce everywhere, though to a lesser extent than twenty years ago, local whites, mulattos and foreigners (French, English, Lebanese, Canadian, American) tend to be in control. In many cases commercial companies are foreign-owned. Even in Haiti there is a tendency for the light-coloured mulattos to control the wealth of the country as well as French, Italians and Lebanese. So although there is no legal discrimination against the coloured man, he often in practice finds himself in a position of social and economic inferiority which appears to be linked with the colour of his skin. Naturally such a situation produces resentment, rancour and bitterness which, when the victim is a writer, often overflows into his writing, whether he is thinking of himself or of his kind. To this should be added the fact that all over the Caribbean the working masses, i.e. the people at the bottom of the economic and social scale, are black and often colour-resentment and class-resentment are blended.

We shall see that the Caribbean intellectual, almost always of middle class, but in some cases of very humble origins, when he turns to writing about the society in which he lives, takes as a target of his attacks that section of people which has placed him and his fellows in a situation of social inferiority. How eloquent in this context is the dedication of the Martinican novelist, Joseph Zobel, in his *La Rue Cases Nègres* (Paris, 1950): 'A ma mère, domestique chez les blancs'—To my mother, a servant in the white people's house. There are various reactions of the coloured writer to the colour situation within his own society. First of all, there is the analysis of relationships with white people, local or foreign. The Martinican novel *Je suis martiniquaise* by Mayotte Capécia, strongly autobiographical in tone, tells of the relationship of a coloured girl with an officer of the French Army during the Second World War. After living with her for two years and giving her a child, the officer leaves Martinique and the authorities will not allow her to go with him. Later he writes to her from France announcing that he is going to marry a French woman; she is left at the end of the book scorned by her own people, who accuse her of betraying her race. In the midst of this plight, she exclaims: 'I wanted to get married, but to a white man. But a coloured woman can never be quite respectable in the eyes of a white man, even if he loves her. I knew it.'[1]

The Barbadian, Slade Hopkinson, in 'Archibald Q. Morris' paints the portrait of a white planter giving a sarcastic account of his prejudice and general way of thinking:

He is a gentleman and the soul of honour.
Attesting by this:

(a) being content with his splendid idleness
(b) being content with his labourers' splendid industriousness
(c) having been at pains to be born white
(d) thereby having, while yet in foetal innocence, assured himself of membership of the proper clubs.[2]

But the poem, in spite of its light, jocose tone ends angrily with the exclamation 'pustula'. In another poem of the same volume Hopkinson, in a dialogue between two white girls, emphasises their superficiality and prejudices. One is explaining why she has changed boy-friends: 'Besides, his grandfather is not white. I only found out last week. I dare not tell Daddy. What a disgrace. But while you were away I met another. This one is definitely pure.'[3]

There are many variations on this theme of the racial problem involving the white society, local or foreign. At a different level, Nicolás Guillén has expressed the situation very succinctly in 'Guadeloupe, W.I.':

The Negroes, working
round the ship. The Arabs, selling.
The French, strolling about and relaxing,
and the sun burning. . . .[4]

And in 'Cane':

The Negro
in the cane-field.
The Yankee
over the cane-field.
The land

> under the cane-field.
> Our blood
> flowing away from us.[5]

Foreign (white) exploitation and exploitation by local whites provide, as we have seen, extremely strong emotional stimulants in the Caribbean. Another social situation in the Caribbean which has found an outlet in literature is the relationship between Negroes and mulattos, for in many Caribbean territories the mulatto tends to identify himself with the whites or tries to set up a separate mulatto society or exclusive social layer, within which the mulatto can enjoy certain privileges. Many mulattos avoid at all costs being confused with the mass of poor Negroes, and they use their light colour (sometimes they can 'pass for white') as a means of gaining social and economic advantages. They are usually attacked with the weapons of ridicule rather than through expressions of hatred, but occasionally they are also the object of impassioned vituperation.

Let us examine two situations involving Negro-mulatto relationships. The first in Haiti, a 'black' republic since 1804, but where a relationship of rivalry has developed between Negroes and mulattos, this 'unfortunate question of the blacks and the mulattos' as Catts-Pressoir has called it. In his *Nation haïtienne*, Dantès Bellegarde writes the following in reference to Dessaline's Constitution of 1805, according to which all Haitians fall under the denomination of 'Negro': 'But unfortunately a constitutional text cannot suppress a social prejudice, and this prejudice continues to cause great damage in Haitian society and has been the source of countless misfortunes for our country'.[6] And Jean Price-Mars, intellectual guide of the generation of the American occupation, and whose influence is still strong, expresses himself with offensive violence in writing of the mulattos of Haiti: 'Just look how some of the most representative figures of our society glory in some bastard filiation. All the abuses of colonial times, the anonymous shame of chance meetings, the result of two sexual orgasms have become titles of pride and social consideration.'[7] It is difficult to be more deeply insulting to a sector of the society of a country. And yet Léon Damas of French Guiana is scarcely less virulent in his denunciation of the mulattos, whom he accuses of making impossible a true Caribbean poetry! In the introduction to his *Poètes d'expression française* he writes: 'From the day when the black proletariat, exploited in the Caribbean by a parasitic bunch of mulattos [*mulâtraille*] who have sold out to the degenerate whites, breaks this double yoke—there will be a Caribbean poetry.'[8] And he shoots another poisoned dart at the mulatto intellectual accusing him of sleeping with his black servant although when he set pen to paper 'he puts himself in a white man's skin'.

The other case is that of the Jamaican, Marcus Garvey. Garvey's action and political thought throw a very significant light on the literature of the Caribbean and give proof that what is expressed by poets and novelists is not just a literary figment but a faithful translation of the emotional reality and indeed aspirations of many coloured men in the Caribbean. Now Garvey did not accept mulattos in his organisation, the Universal Negroes Improvement Association (U.N.I.A.). He regarded them as potential traitors to the black race, people in whom the Negro could have no confidence because of their equivocal position. He treated them as 'time-serving, boot-licking agents of subserviency to the whites', and he accused them of always escaping from their race.

I believe in racial purity, and in maintaining a high standard of racial purity. I am proud I am a Negro. It is only the so-called coloured man (mulattos) who talks of social equality. We do not seek social equality. We do not seek intermarriage. We want the right to have a country of our own where we can foster and re-establish a culture and a civilisation exclusively ours.[9]

The following are three very typical examples of literature ridiculing the attitude of racial snobbery of the mulatto. The first is a short story entitled 'Gan-Gan' by the Trinidadian, Ernest A. Carr, which deals with a middle-class Trinidadian woman, whose mother is black although she herself can pass for white, thanks in part to the art of make-up. Her husband is white. She sends her son to spend some time in the country with his black grandmother with whom the child is happy, partly due to the relief from nervous tension and because the old woman tells him wonderful stories. When he returns home, he proudly announces at a children's party that his grandmother had been a slave. His mother is greatly humiliated and the ladies of 'white' society are terribly shocked. One 'pallid lady' crosses his name off a list of children to be invited to another party in her house.[10] Carr, in this story, certainly ridicules the pretensions of Trinidad near-white society, but at the same time there is a certain element of pity, for the continuous play-acting they engage in has made them unhappy. The middle-class house with its artificiality and nervous tension is contrasted with the natural simplicity of the black grandmother, hidden away out of sight in the country. In 'Civil Strife', also by Carr, we find the case of a coloured woman married to an Englishman. She has developed a pathological repugnance for people of her own colour. The ironical part of the story is that her husband whom she has married to 'whiten' herself is greatly attracted to coloured people and what most attracts him in her physical type is her negroid appearance.[11] Again, the mulatto is presented as artificial, unhappy and absurd while the black characters, who accept themselves for what they are, and the unprejudiced whites appear normal.

In our third example, the play *Vejigantes*[12] by the Puerto Rican, Francisco Arriví, we find a situation very similar to that of Carr's 'Gan-Gan'.

A middle-class mulatto woman who can pass for white if she hides her hair (for this reason she always wears a turban) wants to marry her daughter, who in appearance is completely white, to a young man from the south of the United States. She is the same mulatto woman we saw in Carr's stories, nervous, unsure of herself, slightly unbalanced and socially ambitious. Also in Arriví's play, the old black mother is not ashamed of her colour although she is kept out of sight in a back room, and appears as the healthy, sensible element in the play. The grand-daughter, too, is quite balanced and she finally rejects the life of lies and pretence into which her mother is trying to push her.

The message of both Carr's and Arriví's works is clear: to show up the absurdity of social pretensions based on colour and also to demonstrate the unhappiness and neuroses these can produce. A short story by the Jamaican Hugh Morrison[13] shows the tragic side to the mulatto's problem. A mulatto who has spent many years in the United States has returned to Jamaica to be with 'his people' and to get away from the artificial life led by mulattos in the United States; but he is violently and aggressively rejected by a black shopkeeper.

However, on the whole, snobbery based on more or less light

shades of skin-colour tends to be treated, even if scornfully, with
a certain humour, as is Nicolás Guillén's poem 'Mulata':

> Now I know, mulatto girl
> mulatto girl, now I know what you say
> that my nose
> is like the knot in a tie.
>
> But let me tell you
> you are not so much better,
> because you have a big, big mouth
> and your wool is red.
>
> So smart, with your body
> so smart,
> so smart with your mouth
> so smart;
> so smart with your eyes,
> so smart—
>
> But if I told you the truth
> mulatto girl
> I have enough with my black girl
> and I have no need of you.[14]

The attractive mulatto girl as an object of desire evokes, as
we have seen, universal admiration.

The old prejudices against coloured people have not yet died
in the Caribbean, particularly in the islands which are nearest
to a colonial past, but with the passage of time they have become
largely shade prejudices which none the less produce resentment,
anger and protest as well, often, as a feeling of inferiority. This
is the case in the British and French islands. However, in Cuba,
which has been an independent republic for over sixty years,
feeling about racial discrimination is very bitter. Independence
did not bring the hoped-for equality of opportunity for all
Cubans, and the Negro tended to remain at the very bottom of
the social and economic scale—as a labourer in the plantations,
or doing menial work in the cities. In 1912 this feeling found
expression in a Negro uprising known in Cuban history as 'la
guerra de los negritos', which was staged by disappointed veter-
ans of the War of Independence against Spain but which was
savagely crushed. Two of the most bitter and hopeless works
involving the plight of the Negro in a mixed society are *The
Skin* by Alfonso Hernández Catá and the novel *The Sad Race* by

Jesús Masdeu Reyes, both Cubans. *The Skin* tells of the martyr-dom of a Negro intellectual named Eulogio from 'Taiti' (a fictitious country with a name very like Haiti and an atmosphere which is completely Cuban) who is rejected by the whites because he is black, and by the Negroes of his country who feel that he is not quite one of them because of his superior educa-tion. On account of his skin, his 'cursed pigmentation', he is rejected by both sides, and dies the victim of a political plot in which his own people have had a hand. The tragedy of the hero of *The Skin* is that of a coloured man in a country where coloured people are generally poor and illiterate and who has received an education which has made of him a man of culture, sensibility and honour. His own people consider him a dreamer which, as Hernández Catá puts it, 'in that country is a euphemism for calling a man a fool'.[15] The local Negro politicians want him to decorate their platform, but they do not want his idealism. Eulogio's disappointment with the black politicians is complete and he reflects sorrowfully:

All they could think of was wearing hats, powdering their faces white, secretly accepting bribes which he rejected, justifying at every step the accu-sation of being imitative monkeys which the race that oppressed them made. One could feel in the Negro leaders envy for the bribes, corruption and rackets from which the whites made money.[16]

This cruel story, one of Hernández Catá's best, probes deeply into the confused psychology of many Caribbean Negroes. In *The Sad Race* Jesús Masdeu Reyes (Havana, 1924) gives an 'aggressively sincere' picture of the sufferings of a cultured Negro, again caught between the two races. As a medical doctor the society of his home-town will not allow him to practise his profession, and when finally he is reduced to begging and alco-holism, a group of Negroes suggest he should be put in a lunatic asylum. Masdeu depicts the Negroes as cowardly and syco-phantic, resigned to be treated as inferiors. Like *The Skin* it is a cruel book which leaves a taste of disgust in the mouth at the vileness of men, both black and white.

In all West Indians, skin colour or shade is an inevitable factor in the formation of their psychology, although of course they may react in various ways to the fact of their colour or shade in their relation to a society which is profoundly preoccupied with such questions. It is natural, therefore, that the novelist, as an observer of society, should take into account this factor when he sets out to depict the social and psychological patterns formed by this society.

In *Morning at the Office* (London, 1949), a novel by the Guianian writer, Edgar Mittelholzer, we find one of the most successful examinations of the complicated mechanism of social-racial tensions in Trinidad. To demonstrate this situation, Mittelholzer describes schematically the life of various characters working in a typical Trinidad office, from the Director, who is English, to the office-boy, a young Negro who reads Shakespeare and dreams of becoming Governor of the island. It is a cross-section of Trinidad life, and in each case the character's outlook is determined to a considerable extent by his racial status.

*In the Castle of my Skin* (London, 1953) by the Barbadian George Lamming, is greatly preoccupied with colour problems which perplex the main character, a black boy of very humble extraction, whose growing-up is the subject of the novel. This book is remarkably similar in many ways to the autobiographical novel of the Martinican writer Joseph Zobel, *Rue Cases Nègres*. Yet another aspect of the race and colour theme has appeared in Caribbean literature in the form of emigration novels. West Indian emigration to Europe or the United States is of comparatively recent date; for, although Puerto Rican emigration to the United States dates back to the 1930s, large-scale emigration to England and France from the British and French West Indies started only in the period beginning in 1945, and to the date of writing is still increasing. All the novels to be discussed here were published after 1950.

The West Indian emigrant leaves his country because of economic frustration resulting from overpopulation in relatively small, under-developed territories. Indeed, the overriding impression derived from the novels dealing with West Indian immigrants in New York, London and Paris is that they would go home if they could find equivalent opportunities for making a satisfactory living. Mostly they are unhappy in their new surroundings. The climate, living conditions, and general social atmosphere are felt to be unfavourable, even inimical. For many there is also the problem of racial discrimination and prejudice. Three of the novels under discussion here follow a similar pattern. One or more West Indians arrive either by sea or air in the country where they intend to settle. The period of the voyage is used by the characters to divulge something of their past history and to express the hopes and ambitions to be achieved in the countries for which they are bound. Even the short air trip from Puerto Rico to New York is used for this purpose. This is a device, then, to tell the reader something about the personality and psychology of the main characters, and these traits to some extent foreshadow the subsequent development and behaviour of the characters once they have entered their new environments. The authors are also able in this way to show what their characters were like before the experience of the impact upon them of their new countries. After arrival the various characters go their separate ways, though they tend to meet again later. They also tend to become involved constantly with other West Indians and with people of their adopted countries. But the pattern of relationships after arrival is simple or even over-simplified in some novels while in others, particularly in those of George Lamming, it is rich and complex.

The first of the four novels to be discussed here is *Tropico en Manhattan* (San Juan, 1951) by the Puerto Rican, Guillermo Cotto-Thorner. His approach is essentially sociological: it is a study of the Puerto Ricans living together in New York and their various attempts at adjustment to the alien patterns of life. The characters are divided schematically into the successful and unsuccessful immigrants, i.e. those who go about the problem of adjustment in the right way and those who go about it in the wrong way. The hero Marcos Villalobos, his Puerto Rican girl friend Miriam, Antonio and his wife Fini, are all sensible, balanced people with no dreams of 'getting-rich-quick' through rackets; their attitude to Americans is thoughtful and free from prejudice. Aurelio Fontes ('Yeyo') and Lencho Ortiz, on the other hand, are misfits because they have the wrong approach. Yeyo has come to New York as an adventurer, on the lookout for a way of making abundant and easy money. Lencho is embittered; he suffers from an acute inferiority complex and refuses to try to learn English. He despises his American co-workers and resents what he regards as their discrimination against him. It is pointed out to him by one of the 'good' characters that his unpopularity is partly his own fault since he has never made any attempt to be friendly with Americans and knows nothing about them. Even the more balanced characters are sensitive to the prejudice against Puerto Ricans. The intellectual, Juan Marcos Villalobos, believes that the only way to stop Americans from looking down on Puerto Ricans is for the Puerto Ricans to improve themselves in the terms of their own culture.

> Socially and culturally what are we to them? Just trash. They regard us as barbarians, as uneducated, backward, little better than savages. So, just as we must fight for our economic betterment, it is also our duty to strive to raise our cultural prestige in the eyes of the American people.[17]

His solution, then, is for Puerto Ricans to become conscious of their own cultural values, of which they often are not aware, and to present themselves to Americans with their own cultural identity. To attain this end he founds a Puerto Rican cultural association, the Club Hostos, where lectures on Puerto Rican culture and recitals of music by good Puerto Rican performers are given.

By becoming aware of their own cultural tradition and values and then using them as a means of preserving their separate cultural identity, he maintains, Puerto Ricans will bring about an all-round improvement of status in their relations with the Americans. There is no question to him of assimilation, of becoming American. He presents Puerto Ricans in New York as clinging desperately to their language. Referring to the long letters they write home, he says: 'These letters are an escape valve, an expression of a subjective reality, a revenge on the cosmopolitan atmosphere of the city in which the Puerto Rican feels himself under the constant threat of losing his language and traditions.'[18] He is aware also of the hybrid nature of Puerto Rican culture, and while not utterly rejecting the American side of it, he is insistent on strengthening its Puerto Rican or Hispanic element. He sees this mixed character as a factor of disorder and confusion in the Puerto Rican mind. Rather bitterly, he exclaims: 'By being politically American and of Spanish blood and tradition, we are neither "*gringos*" nor "*jíbaros*" but an undefined mixture of characteristics which are sometimes conflicting.'[19] It is worth mentioning that in this novel scarcely any American figures appear. There is a brief episode between the newly arrived Villalobos and an American girl whose casualness and lack of modesty shocks him. But apart from this and Lencho's unsatisfactory relations with his American co-workers who call him 'spic' and 'jerk', there is no contact at all, either with Americans or other Latin-Americans. The study is kept within the precints of a rather closed Puerto Rican colony, and the Americans remain abstractions throughout.

La fête à Paris (Paris, 1953) by Martinique's Joseph Zobel, starts when the hero, José Hassam, goes aboard a French liner in Martinique bound for France. The first two or three pages, dealing with the voyage, state the main themes which are to be reiterated throughout the book: the relation of black and white (which Zobel writes with capitals), the effect of colonialism on both, a general attack on the cultural values of the French in particular, and, by extension, of western Europe. The tone is sarcastic and sneering. Of the people Hassam meets in France, there is hardly a pleasant Frenchman. The sympathique characters are other French West Indians, Africans, Indo-Chinese, Arabs and a Hungarian girl. All these are united in their hatred of French-colonialism and their suspicious (when not aggressive) reaction to Western civilisation. Of the Hungarian girl it is claimed rather naïvely that 'being Hungarian she has not got her mind loaded with colonialism'.[20]

In order to introduce a critique of Western values, Zobel has created a French character, Jean-Claude Pelletier, who embodies the French line on racial and cultural superiority and with whom Hassam has frank, if somewhat stagy, discussions. Pelletier finally admits that Hassam has triumphed over 'white' civilisation. He has absorbed it while refusing to be absorbed by it. 'On a moral and intellectual plane', he admits, 'you possess all that we had believed we had the monopoly of, even more. You shine with our culture and you do not give a damn about it at the same time. Our prejudices crumble miserably before you. You don't seem to be interested in our money.'[21] The fresh, uncontaminated source of Negro creativeness is contrasted with the decadence of Europe. As one European character is made to say: 'Ah, you do not know what it is to have life and richness, while your masters are declaring their bankruptcy and are realising that they are in their death-throes.'[22] The superior exuberance of the Negro, his zest and appetite for life, are frequently stressed. Even the behaviour of French crowds on festival days is noted by

José Hassam as being dull and uninspired. The movement of the people in the streets on Bastille Day is described as 'a sort of fluid movement—without tone or rhythm. And this incapability of being gay, that is, to be snatched out of the daily routine, thrown out of reality.'[23] Even Hassam feels influenced by the prevailing dullness and has lost much of the 'amplitude and brilliance of his laughter'. Winter seems to be used almost symbolically (Hassam arrives in Paris in mid-winter), and its depressing effects are referred to constantly. For example: 'Even after two years in Paris I find snow austere. That white, thick matter over everything. More austere than if it were black.'[24] As opposed to his loathing for the French and their whole culture, we find Hassam falling into a sort of ecstasy of enthusiasm when he meets the first African he has ever known. His style, which is completely unelevated on the whole, becomes on this occasion, poetic.

> Ousmane Diop was a man of Africa.
> Ousmane Diop, standing in his scarlet bath-robe, had the hieratic beauty of a totem standing in the centre of a village.
> Ousmane Diop, seated in his scarlet, green-fringed dressing-gown, had the serene majesty of a good king in all his splendour.[27]

This, then, is what we find in this novel: firstly, the experiences of a coloured colonial in the course of his adaptation to metropolitan life; secondly, a critique of the culture of the metropolis and the assertion of a different cultural identity based on *négritude*, i.e. the consciousness of the racial-cultural identity all over the world; and thirdly, a critique of French colonialism which, it is suggested, quite apart from its economic exploitation of the colonies, has tried to pervert the true nature of Negroes by turning them into imitation Frenchmen.

There is nothing new in Zobel's aggressive assertions of Negro cultural values or in his harping on the theme of the decline in the creative energy of the white race. These ideas are to be found in other French West Indian writers, notably in Aimé Césaire, Léon Damas, Lionel Attuly and the Haitians Jacques Roumain and Jean Brierre. The theory or the mystique of the creative superiority of the Negro is found in some non-French West Indian writers, although less frequently, and nowhere with such dogmatic force. The exuberance, the capacity for frank, rich enjoyment of the more sensuous aspects of life, are referred to by other West Indians, notably the Jamaican expatriate Claude McKay in such books as *Banjo* (1929), *Home to Harlem* (1937), and *A Long Way from Home* (1937). And also in the early works of the Puerto Rican Luis Palés Matos, such as *Tun Tun de pasa y grifería* (1936) written under the acknowledged influence of Oswald Spengler's *Decline of the West*. What is most striking about Zobel's novel on the experiences of a West Indian immigrant is its overwhelming, obsessive, almost exclusive concern with racial problems.

*Lonely Londoners* (London, 1956) by the Trinidadian, Samuel Selvon, deals with a group of West Indians, mostly from Trinidad. To Selvon the most prominent feature of the immigrant problem is the cohesion of the group. The West Indians are depicted as living among their own people, associating, except for female contacts, with each other and other coloured people. They do not appear to stray much outside the group, although Selvon does not show them at work where they have presumably a wider range of contacts. In their leisure time they return to their group, rather defensively. Although most of Selvon's characters seem to like London—'their London', the little world of the West Indian colony—they find the British unfriendly, even hostile. There is little actual friction, but the environment is felt to be hostile and when it does impinge on the lives of West Indians it is usually in an unpleasant form—colour prejudice, cold-shouldering, giving of heavy, dirty work. Selvon is by no means obsessed with race, as is Zobel, but he shows a sensitiveness about it which certainly influences the lives and outlooks of his characters. For example, one of them reflects after a child has said to its mother, 'Look at that black man!':

> Lord, what is it we people do in this world to have to suffer so? What is it we want that white people and them find it so hard to give? A little work, a little food, a little place to sleep. We are not asking for the sun or the moon. We only want to get by, we don't even want to get on.[26]

The novel, written entirely in a modified form of Trinidad dialect, sufficiently English to be understandable but retaining much of the flavour of Trinidad speech, is made up of a series of incidents and anecdotes, many of them humorous, with little attempt at emotional or psychological depth. It is essentially, to use Selvon's words, 'the kiff-kiff laughter.. the ballad.. the episode, the what-happening'. But it is very much alive, not weighed down by obtrusive discussions. If there is any message at all, it seems to be that the West Indians are out of place in London. The one serious character, symbolically called Moses, whose house is a centre for West Indians and where they go on Sunday mornings, as if going to church, to talk about home, is found at the end of the novel standing on the bank of the Thames making up his mind to go home and reflecting on:

> ...a great aimlessness, a great restless swaying movement that leaving you standing in the same spot. As if a forlorn shadow of doom fall on all the spades in the country. As if he could see the black faces bobbing up and down in the millions of white, strained faces, everybody hustling along the Strand, the spades jostling in the crowd, bewildered, hopeless.[27]

It is not quite clear whether the 'aimlessness', the 'restless swaying', apply just to the West Indians and 'spades', disoriented in a white world which rejects them and to which they cannot really adapt themselves, or whether the passage has overtones of a more general existentialist anguish. The feeling, in any case, springs from his own contemplation of the West Indian set to which he belongs. The constant skimping and scraping for a living which Selvon depicts throughout the book seems to suggest that he does not approve of large numbers of West Indians trying to settle in England. They are essentially, almost tragically, on the surface, living off the country but never basically part of it.

*The Emigrants* (London, 1954) by George Lamming, is the most difficult of the four novels to discuss in the context of this study; for although it deals with a heterogeneous group of West Indians who have got to know each other on the boat coming over and whose subsequent lives in London become closely interwoven, the complex pattern of relationships and the psychological depth of Lamming's vision make it difficult to pick out definite trends. To Lamming neither the characters themselves nor the problems of their adjustment to the new situation created by emigration are simple; and he does not try to simplify, but rather to capture the rich web of interrelationships, personalities and atmosphere in their true complexity. The Puerto Rican, Cotto-Thorner, and the French West Indian, Zobel, have intellectualised the predicament of the immigrant into apparently simple types and categories. This is much easier for the novelist, and also for the reader. But Zobel's abstractions do not come to life; they only theorise and make speeches. Cotto-Thorner's novel contains a thesis on Puerto Rican culture which is stated and discussed almost in essay form; Selvon's novel is neither discursive nor abstract, but he seems to have refrained deliberately from going much beneath the surface of the anecdote. In contrast the result of Lamming's ambitious and largely successful attempt to catch the shifting, fleeting and essentially living complexity of the situation is a piece of literature rather than a pamphlet or an essay. The difficulties encountered by Lamming's West Indians in London seem to derive mainly from the temperamental disaffinities with the English character. They also resent the inability or unwillingness of the English to understand and appreciate them for what they are. Among the impressions of the freshly arrived West Indians on the boat train to London, we find the following, written in modified Barbadian dialect, clearly intended to express the feelings of the ordinary West Indian:

Look Lilian look de ol' geyser in de corner like de whole worl' come to a standstill—he eyes don't wink when he pull that pipe an' he lookin' only Gawd knows where he lookin' like he ain't got eyes in his head—is the way they is in dis country—no talk till you talk, no speak till you speak. No notice till you notice, no nothin' till you somethin'—'tis what ah mean when ah says England.[28]

Again, we find another character explaining the reasons for his resentment against the English, also at a popular, that is, a nonintellectual level:

But even take the English. My feeling for them wus no hate, not real hate, 'cause when I come to think of it, if they'd just show one sign of friendship, just a little sign of appreciation for people like me an' you who from the time we were born, in school an' after school, we wus hearin' about them, if they could understand that and be different, then all the hate you talk 'bout would disappear.[29]

Perhaps the main source of annoyance to the West Indians is what they feel to be the stiffness, the stodginess and unrelaxed nature of many of the English. This feeling of strained, uncomfortable relations comes to a head in a comic scene in the house of Pearson, a particularly stodgy Englishman, where tension, due

to restraint, awkwardness and complete temperamental dis-
harmony becomes so strong that Collis, a West Indian, takes
refuge in the lavatory where he stays a long time, unable to bear
the strain of being with Mr. Pearson and his wife. When
eventually he returns, he thinks: 'He would have liked to kick
him in the stomach, not in anger, but as a way of evoking some
genuine emotion. Only violence could make Mr. Pearson feel.'[30]
Lamming, then, has not overgeneralised his picture of West
Indians attempting to adjust to the semi-alien atmosphere of
London in terms of colour, colonial attitudes, or cultural differences. His characters, both English and West Indian (and he is
the only one of the four novelists who has important 'native'
characters in his book), are individuals with their personal
neuroses and difficulties—although broad, basic temperamental
divergences from the English are suggested. The main problem
is the clash between the restraint, reserve and introversion of the
English and the more easy-going, relaxed, and expansive nature
of the West Indians.

Worth mentioning also is the figure of the idealised African
which we have already observed in Zobel. The African, Azi (a
more subtle character than Zobel's Ousmane Diop), comes and
goes mysteriously among the West Indians, perplexing and enig-
matic. Azi is a mathematical genius. He has taken his 'first degree
with honours in his second year' at Cambridge; he completes his
thesis in two years. And Cambridge regards him as a genius
('Of course they can hardly afford to lose him. They're more
interested in him than in any of them'). Yet Azi has discovered
that he is not really interested in mathematics. Then we find him
giving an impotent English intellectual a magic powder con-
cocted out of a bull's testicles while the intellectual's Lesbian
wife dances around the room in suggestive underwear as Azi
murmurs magic incantations. Yet it is Azi who is presented as a
man with the most profound understanding of life. His letters to
another character, Andrews, clearly are meant to convey a
'philosophy' which is really an uncritical mixture of D. H.
Lawrence and Zen Buddhism. Trite and muddled as this 'philosophy' may be, nevertheless it is clearly intended to be profound
and is attributed to Azi, the idealised African.[31]

It may be too much to say on the basis of two novels (there are
also Africans in Selvon's *Lonely Londoners*) that Africans exer-

cise a sort of fascination for West Indian writers. Nevertheless, when the idealised treatment of African characters by Lamming and Zobel is seen in relation to the existence of Africa as a common theme in West Indian literature, this fact assumes significance. Perhaps it is pertinent that in a much earlier 'expatriate' West Indian novel, *Banjo* (1929) by the Jamaican, Claude McKay, which deals with the adventures of a mixed West Indian and African set on the waterfront in Marseilles, a similar fascination for the African exists. A West Indian character says that he loves to hear the African dialects which 'tasted like brown, unrefined sugar—Sossou, Bambara, Woloff, Fula, Dindo'. McKay states further that the African working-class Negroes are superior to those of the West Indies and America. They are more 'primitive' and less 'savage'.[32]

Apart from the importance of these novels of immigration as pictures of how the large and growing West Indian communities abroad live, basically a sociological interest, and apart from their purely literary interest as narrative and character-drawing, it would seem that this new departure in West Indian literature has produced, and is likely to produce further, two important results. First, it will tend to deliver novelists from the obvious temptations of local colour, general folksiness and 'rurality' to which West Indian writers at home are prone. Writing about West Indians in London, New York or Paris will make them aware of a greater complexity of human relationships than those that exist in the small town, village, or completely rural environment of the West Indian islands. And the second result is that a clearer realisation of the West Indian character is itself likely to emerge as the West Indian writer is confronted in London, New York, or Paris with something so different from what he is used to. There will certainly be a gain in the author's critical awareness of himself as a West Indian, which will help towards a clearer consciousness of West Indian values in a sphere which is badly in need of definition.

It must be realised that the manifestations of the part played by race and colour in the social and psychological make-up of the Caribbean that we have examined are only specimens of a general tendency which abounds in novels, poems, short stories and plays. But this aspect of the race and colour problem is also one of the most lively and realistic. Africanism and the construction of a 'Negro' civilisation on the basis of African values and a racial *mystique* are to a large extent a matter of emotional speculation. The social and psychological problems created by the racial polychromia of the Caribbean belong to everyday life, a constant adjustment of the individual to the society he lives in, and as such are likely for many years to come to constitute a rich vein of literary raw material.

# CONCLUSION

IN the foregoing chapters we have seen something of the extent and scope of the theme of race and colour in the literatures of the Caribbean and although the same theme exists to varying degrees in the literature of other Latin American countries, particularly in Brazil, nowhere does it have the same vitality and complexity. The theme clearly has its roots in the history and social structure of the Caribbean, and such aspects of the theme as the Cuban anti-slavery novels, works dealing with economic and psychological problems or protesting against racial discrimination, are perhaps its simplest manifestations and at the same time constitute a link with a generalised tendency in Latin America towards a literature of militant social protest.

On the other hand, Africanising Africanism and Creole Africanism are more original cultural phenomena and constitute a curious and exotic province on the map of Latin American culture.

We have also observed an attempt, in Afro-Cubanism, to take the Negro as the basis for a sort of Caribbean indigenism. It is quite obvious that the Negro is no more 'indigenous' in Cuba, Haiti, Jamaica etc. than the white Creole; nevertheless he appears more distinctive, more typical, less European and more of the land, and he undeniably gives Caribbean life its particular tonality. This search for a differential element in the way of life, the culture, even language and style of a particular section of the population has been a basic and persistent feature of Latin American culture since the beginning of the nineteenth century and is perhaps a characteristic of culture in all new countries which wish to proclaim their cultural independence, their distinctive national personality. It is certainly the case with Latin America which has put forward its claims to cultural originality in terms of a different national setting, a different and specific feeling of nature, different collective human types, and sometimes a different language (dialect has most commonly been exploited for this purpose).

The attacks on western European civilisation we have seen,

however, have no parallel in Latin America. In continental America there has indeed been a movement towards the rehabilitation and revaluation of the pre-Conquest Indian cultures and towards a clearer and more sympathetic understanding of the present-day Indian attitude to life. The indigenist novels in Peru, Ecuador and Mexico have protested against the abuses and injustice to which the Indians are subjected and some authors have tended to idealise the sense of communal living and the feeling for the land in certain Indian groups. But there has been no serious attempt to erect a system of cultural values based on an Indian attitude to life which could take the place of Western civilisation. There has been no clearly defined racial mystique, nothing comparable to *négritude*. Needless to say, the strong Africanising tendencies of Haiti and the British and French West Indies are totally absent.

As has been pointed out, the close contact between intellectuals of the British and French Caribbean and Africans in London and Paris and the common struggle against similar colonial systems, are not sufficient to account for the emotional strength of the Africanising tendencies, and our constant references to Marcus Garvey and his 'back to Africa' movement have had as their object emphasis of the fact that Caribbean Africanism has a deep appeal at a popular level. Africanism needed no outside stimuli to manifest itself, since a profound racial preoccupation is present in the history, the subsoil of the folklore and the social ecology of most of the Caribbean islands. Writers like Anténor Firmin, Hannibal Price, Claude McKay, George Padmore, Jean Price-Mars were in the vanguard of the revaluation of African culture long before the nationalist awakening in Africa and before the concept of *négritude* was developed in the Caribbean. As will have been observed from the quotations given, the literary quality of poems, novels and short stories is very variable, and it is quite clear that for many writers content predominates over any stylistic considerations. Indeed, most of these writers seem to be principally concerned with the urgency of expressing their emotional or political attitudes. To say that there is a general indifference to literary quality would, however, be a mistake, as the same sense of urgency of expression that we have observed, impelled writers and particularly poets to seek what they felt were the most effective means of communication.

Nicolás Guillén, from Cuba, for example, has been singularly successful in adapting the manner and rhythms of Afro-Cuban popular songs (*huarachas* and *sones*) and quite apart from his 'message' is rated as one of the most original writers in Latin America. Aimé Césaire, whatever he may claim, is clearly influenced by French Surrealism. He is a great poet in a particular style, and at the same time is a poet concerned with speaking as a Negro. Claude McKay was also a stylist and although much of his poetry suffers from an outmoded poetic idiom, particularly as far as his rhymes are concerned, he has a forcefulness of imagery and an underlying passion which makes him of outstanding value in British West Indian literature. It is also true that his main concern was the predicament of the Negro in the world. With few exceptions (possibly Léon Damas and Regnor C. Bernard) the writers we have discussed are by no means exclusively absorbed by considerations of race and colour. Many, however, have consistently regarded themselves as Negro writers and references to the racial situation in the Caribbean and in the world at large tend to appear with great frequency.

Although it is dangerous to make predictions in literature, it seems likely that a concern for race and colour questions will continue in the Caribbean, particularly in Haiti and the British and French West Indies, where it has always been strongest. In these predominantly Negro territories a growing interest in African culture seems likely, and probably further developments in the direction indicated by *négritude* towards the formulation of an Afro-Caribbean culture may be expected.

# ORIGINALS OF SPANISH AND FRENCH
## POEMS QUOTED

LIONEL ATTULY: 'Je t'écris de Paris'                              *Page 92*

    Elle a parlé, parlé
    Dehors il neigeait dehors le froid
    c'est dommage qu'on ne puisse pas
    vous apporter aussi cela
    avec le reste de la civilisation
    avec les soutien-gorges et les ceintures
    les jarretelles et les sangles
    et la suffisance
    et l'ignorance
    et le mensonge des alliances
    et les paroles
    et tout et tout.

       .    .    .    .    .

    et vous prendre en échange
    vos corps de métal souple et dur
    la dignité de votre silence
    dans le don de la volupté
    vos ventres sacrés espoirs d'une humanité
    J'ai retrouvé ma place au creux de ton épaule
    sur ton sein un vrai sein
    capable de supporter le poids d'une tête d'homme
    d'apaiser la soif de paix d'une bouche d'homme
    de nourrir la faim de volupté d'un cœur d'homme
        sans déserter.

REGNOR C. BERNARD: 'Ecroulement'                              *Page 43*

    Les forêts ne sont plus où chantait et dansait
    la prêtresse inspirée,
    et ne s'allume plus le foyer des dieux lares;
    la Couleuvre sacrée ne dort plus sur la branche du mapou,
    les caïmans sont morts sur les berges des fleuves
    et les sanctuaires profanés où brûlait la lampe éternelle;
    et le Sphynx s'afflige au seuil des déserts.
    Les Pharaons sont troublés au cœur des Pyramides,
    et l'Afrique n'est plus
    ni ses Temples
    ni ses mystères,
    car les Prêtres sont morts,

car les Négriers sont venus,
et les tribus de Congo et du Dahomey et des Aradas
ont connu la morsure des chaînes
et du fouet
et la touffeur voyageuse les cales . . .
Et seul à présent
dans la nuit et le silence des montagnes de St. Domingue,
un chant timide de tambour essaie encore parfois
d'élever
jusqu'aux étoiles
la nostalgie profonde des Transplantés d'Afrique.

'Nègre'                                                      *Page 81*

Un incendie immense que ma souffrance de toujours
et vos ricanements
et votre inhumanité
et vos mépris
et vos dédains
ont allumé au fond de ma poitrine
et qui éclatera un jour comme un volcan
        et vous engloutira.

JEAN BRIERRE: 'Black Soul'                                   *Page 84*

Vous attendez le prochain appel,
l'inévitable mobilisation,
car votre guerre à vous n'a connu que des trèves.

'Le drapeau de demain'.                                      *Pages 47–8*

Des hommes que conduit le bas instinct des bêtes,
S'affublant du nom vain de civilisateurs,
Et se croyant des rois sur toute la planète,
Commandent que le noir marqué par sa couleur,
De par le monde, soit la chose inconsciente,
Un marchepied vivant pour l'ostension,
Qu'il vive dans la nuit, qu'il meure dans la fiente,
Tandis que promenant Civilisation,
Ton flambeau teint du sang de notre race,
Ils se pavaneraient sous des arcs triomphaux.


            .     .     .     .     .                        *Page 81*

Que tous les fiers sommets de l'Ile se confondent
Et qu'en parte d'un coup le seul rugissement
Qui fasse s'écrouler la servitude immonde.
Pour écrire les droits du nègre il faut du sang.

Le peuple cache encore sous des dehors serviles
La rage du vengeur et l'âme du héros.

'Me revoici, Harlem'                                    *Page 23*

> Nous connûmes tous deux l'horreur des négriers—
> Et souvent comme moi tu sens des courbatures
> Se réveiller après les siècles meurtriers,
> Et saigner dans ta chair les anciennes blessures.

CARL BROUARD: 'Nostalgie'                               *Page 72*

> Tambour
> quand tu résonne,
> mon âme hurle vers l'Afrique.
> Tantôt,
> je rêve d'une brousse immense
> baignée de lune,
> où s'échevellent de suantes nudités.
> Tantôt
> à une case immonde
> où je savoure du sang dans des crânes humains.

MANUEL DEL CABRAL: 'Haitiano brujo'                     *Page 38*

> Haitiano brujo
> hace tu vela prieta maravillas,
> tú dices.
> Tengo el destino entre mis manos,
> Sí——
> Haitiano brujo, el Futuro
> prisionera en la llama de tu vela.
> Pero,
> ¿ y tu sonrisa de pobre?

'Música barbara'                                        *Page 38*

> Que siga, negra, que siga,
> el terremoto de tu barriga.
> Carne de aguardiente, cuerpo de bongó,
> reventó la selva, desde tu cintura,
> hasta el paraíso de tu mordedura.

ROUSSAN CAMILLE: 'Les soutiers noirs'                   *Pages 23–4*

> La navire chantait si fort
> dans l'effervescence des cocktails
> et la gloire insoucieuse des rires,
> si rugueuse était la mer
> qui varlopait la conque,
> si précipités étaient les ordres
> vos chansons torturées,
>
> .   .   .   .   .
>
> les mêmes que nous chantions

à cet autre voyage
de la lointaine Afrique
aux îles Atlantiques
où étaient les bras liés
la fatigue et la souffrance.

'Nedjé'                                                            *Page 95*

Tes frêles bras
élevés dans la fumée
voulaient étreindre
des siècles d'orgueil
et des kilomètres de paysages,
tandis que tes pas
sur la mosaïque cirée
cherchaient les aspérités
et les détours des routes de ton enfance.

MAURICE CASSÉUS: 'Tambour racial'                                 *Pages 72-3*

Ah, dis-nous ton grand rythme africain, ta voix nocturne
Oh conique tambour racial.

.    .    .    .    .

et que j'étreigne de toute mon âme ce chant sauvage
que tu dédies à la terre poignardée,
et que, en moi, secrètement j'adore.

AIMÉ CÉSAIRE: 'Aux écluses du vide'                               *Page 45*

Europe
je donne mon adhésion à tout ce qui poudroie le ciel de son
                                                    insolence
à tout ce qui est loyal et fraternel à tout ce qui a le courage d'être
                                                    éternellement
neuf à tout ce qui sait donner son coeur au feu à tout ce qui a
                                                    la force de
sortir d'une sève inépuisable à tout ce qui est calme et sûr
à tout ce qui n'est pas toi
Europe
nom considérable de l'éron.

'Cahier d'un retour au pays natal'                                *Page 58*

Parce que nous vous haïssons vous et
votre raison, nous nous réclamons de la
démence précoce de la folie flambante
du cannibalisme tenace.

.    .    .    .    .                                             *Pages 46, 59*

Eia pour ceux qui n'ont jamais rien inventé

pour ceux qui n'ont jamais rien exploré
pour ceux qui n'ont jamais rien dompté

mais ils s'abandonnent, saisis, à l'essence de toute chose
ignorants des surfaces mais saisis par le mouvement de toute chose
insoucieux de dompter, mais jouant le jeu du monde
véritablement les fils aînés du monde
poreux à tous les souffles du monde
aire fraternelle de tous les souffles du monde
lit sans drain de toutes les eaux du monde
étincelle du feu sacré du monde
chair de la chair du monde palpitant du mouvement même du
    monde.

.    .    .    .    .                                    *Pages 45, 59*

Ecoutez le monde blanc
horriblement las de son effort immense
ses articulations rebelles craquer sous les étoiles dures
ses raideurs d'acier bleu transperçant la chair mystique
écoute ses victoires proditoires trompeter ses défaites
écoute aux alibis grandioses son piètre trébuchement,
pitié pour nos vainqueurs omniscients et naïfs.

.    .    .    .    .                                    *Page 59*

ma Négritude n'est pas une pierre, sa surdité
ruée contre la clameur du jour
ma Négritude n'est pas une taie d'eau
morte sur l'oeil mort de la terre
ma Négritude n'est ni une tour ni une cathédrale
elle plonge dans la chair rouge du sol
elle plonge dans la chair ardente du ciel

.    .    .    .    .                                    *Page 65*

ne faites pas de moi cet homme de haine pour qui je n'ai que haine
car pour me cantonner en cette unique race
vous savez pourtant mon amour tyrannique
vous savez que ce n'est point par haine des autres races
que je m'exige bêcheur de cette unique race
que ce que je veux
c'est pour la faim universelle
pour la soif universelle.

'Pour saluer le tiers monde'                             *Page 76*

Je vois l'Afrique multiple et une
    verticale dans la tumultueuse péripétie
    avec ses bourrelets, ses nodules,

un peu à part, mais à portée
du siècle, comme un cœur de réserve.

Et je redis: Hoo mère
        et je lève ma force
        inclinant ma face.
        Oh, ma terre.
Que je me l'émiette doucement entre pouce et index
Que je m'en frotte la poitrine, le bras
        le bras gauche
Que je m'en caresse le bras droit.

Hoo ma terre est bonne
        avec cet apaisement que donne
        un lever du soleil

Vois:    .   .   .   .   .
        l'Afrique n'est plus
        au diamant du malheur
        un noir cœur qui se strie.

MASSILLON COICOU: 'Le supplice des noirs'                    *Page 26*

Oh, no reprochez pas au nègre ses excès
N'osez pas le maudire et comprenez sa haine.

LÉON DAMAS: 'Ils ont'                                        *Pages 81–2*

Ils ont si bien su faire
si bien faire les choses
les choses
qu'un jour nous avons tout
nous avons tout foutu de nous-mêmes
tout foutu de nous-mêmes en l'air.
Il ne faudrait pourtant pas grand'chose
pourtant pas grand'chose
pour qu'en un  jour tout aille
tout aille
dans le sens de notre race
à nous nous
Il ne faudrait pas grand'chose.

'Limbe'                                                      *Pages 47, 92*

Rendez-les-moi, mes poupées noires
qu'elles dissipent
l'image des catins blêmes marchandes d'amour
qui s'en vont viennent
sur le boulevard de mon ennui.
Rendez-les-moi mes poupées noires que je joue avec elles

les jeux naïfs de mon instinct
rester à l'ombre de ses lois
recouvrer mon courage
mon audace
me sentir moi-même
nouveau moi-même de ce que j'étais hier
    sans complexités
        hier
quand est venu l'heure du déracinement.

'Pour sûr'                                                      *Page 47*

Alors je vous mettrai les pieds dans
le plat
ou bien tout simplement la main au collet
de tout ce qui m'emmerde
en gros caractères
colonisation
civilisation
assimilation et la suite.

'Solde'                                                       *Pages 44–5*

J'ai l'impression d'être ridicule
dans leurs souliers dans leur smoking
dans leur plastron dans leur faux col
dans leur monocle dans leur melon

   .    .    .    .    .

J'ai l'impression d'être ridicule
avec les théories qu'ils assaisonnent
au goût de leurs besoins de leurs passions

   .    .    .    .    .

J'ai l'impression d'être ridicule
parmi eux complice parmi eux souteneur
parmi eux égorgeur les mains effroyablement rouges
du sang de leur civilisation.

GEORGES DESPORTES: 'Auto da fé'                             *Page 67*

Nous nous sommes dépouillés de nos vêtements d'Europe,
En brutes magnifiques et barbares que nous sommes:
Et nous avons dansé tout nus
Tout nus autour des flammes hautes.—

Tout nus autour du grand bûcher de joie
Tout nus sous les palmiers, tout nus sous les bambous
Nous crions sous le ciel des Tropiques;
Au son du jazz puissant des îles Caraïbes
L'orgueil d'être noirs
La gloire d'être nègres.

OSWALD DURAND: 'L'epopée des aïeux'                                    *Page 81*

    Ecoutez. Ecoutez, c'est une autre Iliade.
    Elle eut son noir Achille et son Agamemnon.
    Dans notre cœur le fer burina chaque nom.
    Ce sont des morts vivants. C'est toute une pléiade.

'Nos payses'                                                          *Page 88*

    Si ma muse, un joir me demande
    des vers—une ode, un sonnet—
    d'honneur. Je lui ferai l'offrande
    du plus délicieux couplet.

    Je n'irai pas, quittant le Nouveau Monde,
    monter mon luth pour la blanche aux yeux bleus,
    pour la châtaine, la rousse ou la blonde,
    pâles sous leur ciel nébuleux.
    Mais à ma négresse
    dont la folle caresse
    verse en mon cœur l'ivresse,
    vers aux doux sons
    chansons
    Je chanterai sa lèvre
    qui jamais ne me sèvre
    et qui donne la fièvre
    et ses charmants tourments.

PIERRE FAUBERT: 'La négresse'                                         *Page 88*

    Je suis fier de te le dire, o négresse, je t'aime.
    Et ta noire couleur me plaît. Sais-tu pourquoi?
    C'est que, nobles vertus, chaste cœur, beauté même,
    Tout ce qui me charme enfin, le ciel l'a mis en toi.

    Or d'une absurde erreur, innocente victime
    Mire-toi dans cette onde aux feux naissants du jour;
    Et vois comme tes yeux sont beaux du don sublime,
    Source de dévouement, et que l'on nomme l'amour.

GILBERT GRATIANT: 'Missions'                                          *Page 66*

    La terre est pleine d'arbres
    Et le ciel de tempêtes
    L'eau sourd des chauds humus où la bête s'éveille
    Et le Négre connaît
    Par longue intimité et profond cousinage
    Le langage des eaux parlant avec les astres,
    La volonté du vent et les ordres du feu.

Merci, au nom de l'homme
Pour ta part apportée;
Tes bras étaient chargés
Et pliant le genou
Esclave ou bien guerrier
Tu mis aux pieds du monde
Les fruits de la ferveur et le pouvoir du rythme.

NICOLÁS GUILLÉN: 'Balada de mis dos abuelos'     *Page 37*

Sombras que sólo yo veo
me escoltan mis dos abuelos.

Don Federico me grita,
y Taita Facundo calla;
los dos en la noche sueñan
y andan, andan.
Yo los junto.—
—Federico
Facundo. Los dos se abrazan.
Los dos suspiran. Los dos
las fuertes cabezas alzan;
los dos del mismo tamaño
bajo las estrellas altas;
ansia negra y ansia blanca,
los dos del mismo tamaño
gritan, sueñan, lloran, cantan.
Sueñam, lloran, cantan.
Lloran, cantan.
Cantan.

'Dos niños'     *Page 34*

Dos niños, ramas de un mismo árbol de miseria,
comen en un portal, bajo la noche calurosa.

'Elegía'     *Pages 24–5*

Por el camino de la mar
vino el pirata,
mensajero del Espíritu Malo,
con su cara de un solo mirar,
y con su monótona pata
de palo.
Por el camino de la mar.
Hay que aprender a recordar
lo que las nubes no pueden olvidar.

Por el camino de la mar,
con el jazmín y el toro,

y con la harina y con el hierro,
el negro, para fabricar
el oro;
para llorar en su destierro.
por el camino de la mar.

¿Cómo vais a olvidar
lo que las nubes aun pueden recordar?

Por el camino de la mar,
el pergamino de la ley,
la vara para malmedir,
y el látigo de castigar,
y la sífilis del virrey,
y la muerte, para dormir
sin despertar,
por el camino de la mar.

Duro recuerdo recordar
lo que las nubes no pueden olvidar
por el camino de la mar.

'Madrigal'                                                        *Page 94*
   Tu vientre sabe más que tu cabeza
   y tanto como tus muslos,
   Esa
   es la fuerte gracia negra
   de tu cuerpo desnudo.
   Signo de selva el tuyo,
   con tus collares rojos,
   tus brazaletes de oro curvo,
   y ese caimán oscuro
   nadando en el Zambeze de tus ojos.

'Mi patria es dulce por fuera'                                    *Page 35*
   me quiso dar con la mano
   me quiso dar con la mano
   pero allí se quedó muerto
   bien pero allí se quedó muerto.

'Mulata'                                                          *Page 103*
   Ya yo me enteré, mulata,
   mulata, ya sé que dice
   que yo tengo la narice
   como nudo de corbata.

   Y fíjate bien que tú
   no eres tan adelantá

porque tu boca es bien grande
y tu pasa coloradá.

Tanto tren con tu cuerpo,
tanto tren:
tanto tren con tu boca,
tanto tren:
tanto tren con tu sojo,
tanto tren—

Si tú supiera, mulata,
la verdá:
que yo con mi negra tengo
y no te quiero pa na.

'Sabás'                                                          *Page 34*

Coge tu pan, pero no lo pidas;
Coge tu luz, coge tu esperanza cierta
como a un caballo por las bridas.

SALOMÉ UREÑA DE HENRÍQUEZ: 'Anacaona'          *Page 7*

Región encantadora,
vergel de los amores
que guarda los primores
del primitivo edén.
En sus amenos campos
la paz de la existencia,
sencilla la inocencia
gozar pudo también.

La indígena familia,
la raza de Quisqueya,
de sus comarca bella
en posesión feliz
miraba candorosa
pasar la vida en calma,
sin pesadumbre el alma,
sin yugo la cerviz.

La selva le brindaba
sus frutos regalados,
sus flores los collados,
sus aguas el raudal;
y pródigos, fecundos,
los senos de los mares
de peces a millares
riquísimo caudal.

Ojeda, el español, de alma de acero,
fanático profundo,
audaz y afortunado aventurero
en ardides diabólico.

ALFONSO HERNÁNDEZ CATÁ: 'Los frutos ácidos'        Page 32

Por muy vestida que vaya
la negra estatua se ve
ojos de concha marina
labios de crudo bisté.

La cintura muele deseos
se le escapan palabras extrañas,
cien ojos buscan los caminos
que conducen a sus entrañas.

Africa llora en la orquesta
húmedo sopor domina.
Al latigazo del trópico
el ario orgullo se inclina.

DOMINIQUE HYPPOLYTE: 'Loetitia-La Noire'        Page 89

Sous les avocatiers aux verdoyantes branches
Nous irons savourer l'amour comme un beau fruit.

LÉON LALEAU: 'Trahison'        Page 43

Et ce désespoir à nul autre égal
D'apprivoiser, avec des mots de France,
Ce cœur qui m'est venu du Sénégal.

PAUL LARAQUE: 'Transplanté'        Page 73

Lourd de toute la langueur rapportée du bled
L'angoisse del Griots baignant mes prunelles flétries.
J'ai senti par des nuits d'inquiétude africaine,
J'ai senti l'âme du monde hostile à ma race.

JACQUES LENOIR: 'Nous nègres'        Page 46

Nous n'avons pas colonisé l'Afrique
Nous n'avons pas découvert l'Amérique
nous qui sommes couleur de Satan—

.     .     .     .     .

Nous nous levons et notre dance
c'est la terre qui tourne
notre chant qui rompt la vaisselle du silence
c'est le rythme sans nom des saisons
le carrefour des quatre éléments.

PHILIPPE THOBY MARCELLIN: 'Petite noire'                    *Page 91*
 Bouche épaisse, nez écrasé, elle est bien vilaine, la petite noire,
             bien vilaine.
 Et très noire, comme tous les péchés. Mais tu souris
 Et c'est une fête des anges.
 Douceur de tes regards blancs,
 Candeur de tes dents blanches—
 Je te chanterai, petite noire, c'est bien ton tour.
 Je dirai la grâce de ton corps droit comme un palmiste, mais
           souple comme la flamme.
 Je te dirai ta démarche cadencée et la file indienne parfumée de
     baume et de menthe qui nous apporte des mornes
 Les fruits et les légumes de Kenskoff et de Furcy.

'Sainement'                                               *Pages 45–6*
 Jurant un éternel dédain aux raffinements européens,
 Je veux désormais à vous chanter, révolutions, fusillades, tueries,
 bruit des coco-macaques sur des épaules noires,
 mugissements du lambi, lubricité mystique du voudou,
 vous chanter dans un délire trois fois lyrique et religieux,
 me dépouiller de tous les oripeaux classiques
 et me dresser nu, très sauvage et très descendant d'esclaves,
 pour entonner d'une voix neuve le de profundis
 des civilisations pourrissantes.

PAUL NIGER: 'Je n'aime pas l'Afrique'                      *Page 51*
 Christ racheta l'homme mauvais et bâtit son Eglise à Rome.
 Sa voix fut entendue dans le désert. L'Eglise sur la Société, la
             Société
 sur l'Eglise, l'une portant l'autre
 Fondèrent la civilisation où les hommes, dociles à l'antique sagesse
 pour apaiser les anciens dieux, pas morts,
 Immolèrent tous les dix ans quelques millions de victimes.

 Il avait oublié l'Afrique.
 Mais quand on s'aperçut qu'une race (d'hommes?)
 Devait encore à Dieu son tribut de sang noir, on lui fit un rappel.
    .  .  .  .  .

 Jésus étendit les mains sur ces têtes frisées, et les nègres furent
             sauvés.
 Pas ici bas bien sûr.

LUIS PALÉS MATOS: 'Numen'                                  *Page 78*
 Jungla africana—Tembandumba
 Manigua haitiana—Macandal.
 Es la Nigricia. Baila el negro.

Baila el negro en la soledad.
Atrevesando inmensidades
Sobre el candombe su alma va
Al limbo oscuro donde impera
La negra fórmula esencial.
Dale su fuerza el hipopótamo,
Coraza bríndale el caimán,
Le da sigilo la serpiente,
El antílope agilidad,
Y el elefante poderoso
Rompiendo selvas al pasar,
Le abre camino hacia el profundo
Y eterno numen ancestral.

'Mulata-Antilla'                                             *Page 90*

Eres ahora mulata,
Todo el mar y la tierra de mis islas.
Sinfonía frutal cuyas escalas
Rompen furiosamente en tu catinga.
He aquí en su verde traje la guanabana
Con sus finas y blandas pantaletas
De muselina: he aquí el caimito
Con su leche infantil; he aquí la piña
Con su corona de soprano. Todos
Los frutos, oh, mulata, tú me brindas,
En la clara bahía de tu cuerpo
Por los soles del trópico bruñido.

'Ñam-ñam'                                                   *Page 33*

Asia sueña su nirvana
América baila su jazz,
Europa juega y teoriza.
Africa gruñe: ñam-ñam.

'Pueblo negro'                                           *Pages 32–3*

Mussumba, Tombuctú, Farafangana,
Caserío irreal de paz y sueño.

Alguien disuelve perezosamente
Un canto monorítmico en el viento.

        .      .      .      .      .

Es la negra que canta
Su sobria vida de animal doméstico;
La negra de las zonas soleadas
Que huele a tierra, a salvajina, a sexo.
Es la negra que canta,
Y su canto sensual se va extendiendo

Como una clara atmósfera de dicha
Bajo la sombra de los cocoteros.

REGINO PEDROSO: 'Hermano negro'  *Pages 33–4*

Para sus goces
el rico hace de tí un juguete.
Y en París, y en Neuva York, y en Madrid, y en la Habana,
igual que bibelots,
se fabrican negros de paja para la exportación.

. . . . .

¿No somos más que negro?
¿No somos más que jacará?
¿No somos más que rumba, lujurias negras y comparsas?
¿No somos más que mueca y color?
¿Mueca y color?

. . . . .

Da al mundo tu grito rebelde
tu humana voz—
y apaga un poco tus maracas.

JOSÉ RODRÍGUEZ MÉNDEZ: 'Poemas del Batey'  *Page 25*

El látigo del mayoral nos castigaba los ijares de miedo
para que marcháramos dóciles como potros embridados
junto a los bueyes
moríamos también como bestias
castigados por el aguijón esclavista.

. . . . .

Y para 'consolarnos' de nuestras llagas ulceradas
nos hablaban del Cielo.

Ahora somos esclavos también
porque sudamos y nos desgarramos las manos
por un jornal barato.

JACQUES ROUMAIN: 'Bois d'ébène'  *Page 84*

il sera trop tard je vous dis
car jusqu'aux tam-tams ont appris le langage
de l'internationale
All together
les sales indiens
les sales indochinois
les sales arabes
les sales malais
les sales juifs
les sales propriétaires,
et nous voici debout
tous les damnés de la terre.

. . . . .

POURTANT                                              *Page 66*
je ne veux être que de votre race
ouvriers paysans de tous les pays.


'Guinée'                                              *Pages 74–5*
C'est le lent chemin de Guinée
La mort t'y conduira
Voici les branchages, les arbres, la forêt
Ecoute le bruit du vent dans ses longs cheveux
d'éternelle nuit.

C'est le lent chemin de Guinée
Tes pères t'y attendent sans impatience
Sur la route, ils palabrent
Ils attendent
Voici l'heure où les ruisseaux grelottent
comme des chapelets d'os
C'est le lent chemin de Guinée
Il ne te sera pas fait de lumineux accueil
Au noir pays des hommes noirs:
Sous un ciel fumeux percé de cris d'oiseaux
Autour de l'œil du marigot
              les cils des arbres s'écartent sur la clarté pourrissante
Là, t'attend au bord de l'eau un village paisible,
Et la case de tes pères, et la dure pierre familiale
                        où reposer enfin ton front.


'Nouveau sermon nègre'                               *Page 50*
Nous ne leur pardonnerons pas, car ils savent ce qu'ils font

              .      .      .      .      .

Ils ont fait de l'homme saignant le dieu sanglant
Oh Judas ricane, Oh Judas ricane.

              .      .      .      .      .

Et dans les caves des monastères le prêtre compte les intérêts
des trente deniers.
Non, frères, camarades,
Nous ne prierons plus

              .      .      .      .      .

Nous ne chanterons plus les tristes spirituels désespérés
Un autre chant jaillit de nos gorges
Nous déployons nos drapeaux rouges.


              .      .      .      .      .        *Page 85*
Non, frères, camarades
Nous ne prierons plus

Notre révolte s'élève comme le cri de l'oiseau de tempête au-dessus
du clapotement pourri des marécages
Nous ne chanterons plus les tristes spirituels désespérés
Un autre chant jaillit de nos gorges
Nous déployons nos rouges drapeaux
Tachés du sang de nos justes
Sous ce signe nous marcherons
Sous ce signe nous marchons
Debout les damnés de la terre
Debout les forçats de la faim.

'Surprise'                                        *Pages 50–1, 82*

        Surprise
        Jésusmariejoseph
        quand nous atrapperons
        en riant affroyablement
        le missionaire par la barbe
        pour lui apprendre à notre tour
        à coups de pieds au cul
        que nos ancêtres
        ne sont pas des gaulois
        que nous nous foutons
        d'un Dieu qui
        s'il est le père
        eh bien alors, nous autres, les sales nègres
        faut croire que nous
        ne sommes que ses fils bâtards
        et inutile de gueuler
        jésusmariejoseph
        comme une vieille outre de mensonge débordée
        il faut bien
        que nous t'apprenions en définitive
        de nous prêcher à coups de chicot des confitéors
        l'humilité
        la résignation
        à notre sort maudit
        de nègres, de niggers, de sales nègres.

EMILE ROUMER: 'Marabout de mon cœur'.                *Page 89*

        Marabout de mon cœur aux seins de mandarine,
        tu m'es plus savoureux que crabe en aubergine,
        tu es un afiba dedans mon calalou,
        le doumbreuil de mon pois, mon thé de l'herbe à clou,
        tu es le bœuf salé dont mon cœur est la douane.
        l'accassan au sirop qui coule en ma gargane.

José Z. Tallet: 'Rumba'  *Page 32*

    Y la niña Tomasa se desarticula
    y hay olor a selva
    y hay olor a grajo
    y hay olor a hembra
    y hay olor a macho
    y hay olor a solar urbano
    y olor a rústico barracón.
    Y las dos cabezas dos cocos secos
    en que alguno, con yeso escribiera
    arriba, una diéresis, abajo un guión.
    Y los dos cuerpos de los dos negros
    son dos espejos de sudor.

Daniel Thaly: 'Le jardin des tropiques'  *Page 71*

    N'entends-tu pas un chant lointain et si plaintif
    Qui traîne un pur sanglot dans la nuit tropicale?
    On dirait le soupir des mers sur un récif
    A l'heure où chaque flot expire dans un râle.

    Celui qui chante au loin derrière les maïs,
    Devant la cendre morte au foyer de sa case,
    Est un vieux Congolais qui pleure son pays
    Et que le clair de lune a remis en extase.

    Il n'était rien qu'un mince et dolent négrillon,
    Quand, vêtu seulement d'un pagne vermillon,
    Sur un blanc négrier il passa l'Atlantique.

    Depuis, la nostalgie habite dans son âme:
    Rien ne l'a consolé de sa lointaine Afrique
    Où sont les fleuves bleus chers à l'hippopotame.

# NOTES

*Introduction*

[1] Rodó, J. E., *Hombres de América*, Barcelona, 1920
[2] Portuondo, J. A., *El heroísmo intelectual*, Mexico, 1953, p. 106
[3] Sánchez, Luis Alberto, *Proceso y contenido de la novela hispanoamericana*, Madrid, 1953
[4] Borges, J. L., *Cursos y conferencias*, Buenos Aires, 1953, p. 60

## Chapter I

## THE ANTI-SLAVERY NOVEL IN CUBA: INDIANS AND NEGROES

[1] Cometta Manzino, Aida, *El indio en la poesía de América española*, Buenos Aires, 1939, and Meléndez, Concha, *El indio en la novela hispano-americana*, Madrid, 1934
[2] Henríquez Ureña, Pedro, *Seis ensayos en busca de nuestra expresión*, Buenos Aires, 1926, p. 25
[3] Feijóo, Samuel, 'Sobre los movimientos por una poesía cubana', *Revista Cubana*, June–December 1949, pp. 63–176
[4] Ureña de Henríquez, Salomé, *Poesás completas*, Ciudad Trujillo, pp. 242–3
[5] Ibid, p. 268
[6] Galván, Manuel de Jesús, *Enriquillo*, Buenos Aires 1944, p. 467
[7] Henríquez Ureña, Max, *Panorama histórico de la literatura dominicana*, Rio de Janeiro, 1945, pp. 197–8
[8] In the literature of Haiti, Jamaica, Trinidad and the Lesser Antilles, the Indian, Arawak or Carib have been used by writers though not to the same extent as in the Spanish Caribbean. The Indian poems of the Haitian, Frédéric Burr-Reynaud, in his *Poèmes quisqueyens* (Paris, 1926) for example, reflect a vision of the Indian very similar to that found in the Spanish American poets, an idyllic vision of primitive simplicity. However, the Indian theme can be regarded as secondary in the British and French West Indies.
[9] Rosenblat, Angel, *El desarrollo de la población indígena de América*, Madrid, 1935
[10] Out of the various documents given to him, Madden composed the book entitled: *Poems by a Slave in the Island of Cuba, Recently Liberated. Translated from the Spanish by R. R. Madden M.D. with the History of the Early Life of the Negro Poet Written by Himself to which are Prefixed Two Pieces of Descriptive of Cuban Slavery by R. R. Madden.* The book was published by the Anti-Slavery Society in London in 1840

[11] Suárez Romero, Anselmo, *Francisco*. Edition with prologue by Mario Cabrera Saqui, Havana, 1947. Note 2, p. 180

[12] Ibid, p. 57

[13] Ibid, p. 81

[14] Ibid, pp. 65 and 101

[15] Zambrana, Mario, *Francisco*, Havana, 1951. Note by Armando Muñoz to the first edition.

[16] Ibid, p. 153

[17] Ibid, pp. 37–8

[18] Villaverde, Cirilo, *Cecilia Valdés*, Havana, 1941. Introduction

[19] Ibid, p. 102

[20] See Chapter VIII, 'Social and Psychological Problems'

[21] Op. cit., p. 149

[22] Op. cit., p. 150

[23] Gómez de Avellaneda, Gertrudis, *Sab*, Paris, 1920, p. 21

[24] Ibid, pp. 75–6

[25] Ibid, p. 154

[26] Zambrana, op. cit., p. 158

[27] Martí, José, *Obras completas*, Havana, 1953, p. 489

[28] Ibid, p. 270

[29] Ibid, p. 488

[30] Ibid, p. 487

[31] Senghor, Léopold Sédar, *La nouvelle poésie nègre et malgache*, Paris, 1948, p. 122

[32] Camille, Roussan, *Assaut à la nuit*, Port-au-Prince, 1940

[33] Hopkinson, Slade, *The Four and other Poems*, Barbados, 1954

[34] Guillén, Nicolás, *El son entero*, Buenos Aires, 1947, p. 114

[35] Sanz y Díaz, José, *La lira negra*, Madrid, 1945, p. 89

[36] Coicou, Massillon, *Poésies nationales*, Paris, 1892, p. 60

*Chapter II*

## AFRO-CUBANISM

[1] Varela, J. L., *Ensayos de poesía indígena en Cuba*, Madrid, 1951

[2] Ortiz, Fernando, *Revista Bimestre*, vol. XXXVII, Havana, 1936, p. 26

[3] Marinello, Juan, 'Sobre una inquietud cubana', *Revista de Avance*, February 1930

[4] Marinello, Juan, *Poética, ensayos en entusiasmo*, Madrid, 1933, p. 142

[5] Guirao, Ramón, *Orbita de la poesía afrocubana*, Havana, 1936. Prologue

[6] Ortiz, Fernando, *Revista Bimestre*, vol. XXXVII. Havana, 1936, p. 224

[7] Carpentier, Alejo, *Ecué-Yamba-O*, Madrid, 1933, p. 66

[8] Palés Matos, Luis, *Poliedro*, San Juan, 1927

[9] Palés Matos, Luis, *El mundo*, San Juan, 26 November 1932

[10] Ibid

[11] Tallet, José Z., 'La Rumba' (first published in 1928), Cintio Vitier, *Cincuenta años de poesía cubana*, Havana, 1952, p. 224

[12] Guirao, op. cit., p. 127

[13] Palés Matos, Luis, *Tun tun de pasa y grifería*, San Juan, 1950, p. 63. (First published 1937)

[14] Ibid, p. 51

[15] Pedroso, Regino, *Antología poética*, Havana, 1939, p. 114

[16] Vitier, Cintio, *Cincuenta años de poesía cubana*, Havana, 1952, p. 229

[17] Guillén, Nicolás, op. cit. (First published in *West Indies Ltd.*, 1934)

[18] Ibid, p. 65

[19] Ibid, p. 130

[20] Fernandez de Castro, J. A., *Tema negro en la literatura cubana*, Havana, 1943. Introduction

[21] *Revista Cubana*, January 1946, p. 55

[22] Ortiz, Fernando, *Revista Bimestre*, vol. XXIV, 1934, p. 112

[23] Guillén, op. cit., p. 50. (First published in *West Indies Ltd.*, 1934)

[24] *El Mundo*, San Juan, 19 November 1932

[25] Cabral, Manuel del, *De este lado del mar*, Ciudad Trujillo, 1949. Introduction

[26] Cabral, Manuel del, *Doce poemas negros*, Ciudad Trujillo, 1935, p. 77

[27] Ibid, p. 12

[28] *República Dominicana*, Tomo XI, 'Coleccion Americana', Barranquilla 1954, p. 52

## Chapter III

## REJECTION OF EUROPEAN CULTURE AS A THEME IN CARIBBEAN LITERATURE

[1] Firmin, Anténor, *De l'égalité des races humaines*, Paris, 1885, p. 337

[2] Price-Mars, Jean, *Ainsi parla l'oncle*, Port-au-Prince, 1928, p. 147

[3] Ibid, p. 235

[4] Garvey, Marcus, *Philosophy and Opinions*, New York, 1926, vol. II, p. 19

[5] Garvey, Marcus, *The Tragedy of White Injustice*, New York, 1927, p. 3

[6] Bernard, Regnor C., 'The Fall', Port-au-Prince, 1945, p. 15

[7] Laleau, Léon, *Musique nègre*, Port-au-Prince, 1931, p. 15

[8] McKay, Claude, *Selected Poems*, New York, 1953, p. 41

[9] Damas, Léon, *Pigments*, Paris, 1937

[10] Césaire, *Cahier d'un retour au pays natal*, Paris, 1947. (First published in the review *Volonté*, Paris, 1939, p. 79)

[11] Césaire, *Soleil cou-coupé*, Paris, 1948, pp. 92–3

[12] Marcellin, Philippe Thoby, 'La trouée', 1 July 1927

[13] Césaire, *Soleil cou-coupé*, p. 78

[14] Lenoir, Jacques, 'Nous nègres', *Optique*, Port-au-Prince, 1954, No. 3

[15] Baguidy, Joseph, *Optique*, 1954, No. 4

[16] Damas, Leon, op. cit., 'Pour sûr'

[17] Ibid, 'Limbe'

[18] Brièrre, Jean, *Le drapeau de demain*, Port-au-Prince, 1931, p. 27

[19] Denis, Lorimer and Duvalier, François, 'L'essentiel de la doctrine des Griots', *Les Griots*, vol. 2, No. 2, 1939, p. 153

[20] Ibid, p. 153

[21] Denis and Duvalier, *Psychologie ethnique et historique*, vol. 4, No. 4, 1939

[22] Césaire, *Discours sur le colonialisme*, Paris, 1950, p. 24

[23] Ibid, p. 37

[24] Capécia, Mayotte, *Je suis martiniquaise*, Paris, 1948, p. 65

[25] Roumain, Jacques, *Bois d'ébène*, Port-au-Prince, 1945

[26] Ibid

[27] Niger, Paul, in Senghor, op. cit., pp. 95–6

[28] Piquion, René, *Langston Hughes: un chant nouveau*, Port-au-Prince, 1945, p. 32

[29] Ibid, pp. 32–3

[30] Lemaître, Georges, *From Cubism to Surrealism in French Literature*, Harvard, 1941, p. 76

[31] Palés Matos, Luis, *Poliedro*, 1927

[32] *El Mundo*, 1938

[33] Balaguer, Joaquín, *La realidad dominicana*, Buenos Aires, 1947, p. 117

[34] Sartre, Jean-Paul, *L'Orphée noir*, in Senghor, op. cit., IX

*Chapter IV*

## FRENCH WEST INDIAN BACKGROUND OF *NÉGRITUDE*

[1] Sartre, J.-P., *L'Orphée noir*, in Senghor, op. cit.

[2] Jahn, Janheinz, *Muntu*, London 1961. (First published in German, 1958)

[3] Césaire, Aimé, *Cahier d'un retour au pays natal* (Préface d'André Breton, Paris, 1947), pp. 50–1

[4] Ibid, p. 78

[5] Ibid, p. 79

[6] Ibid, pp. 77–8

[7] Fanon, Frantz, *Peau noire masques blancs*, Paris, 1952, p. 122

[8] Ibid, p. 125

[9] Ibid, p. 131

[10] Sartre, in Senghor, op. cit., p. 27

[11] Césaire, *Les armes miraculeuses*, Paris, 1946, p. 126

[12] See for example Tutuola, Amos, *The Palm-Wine Drinkard*, London, 1952, Senghor, *Chants d'ombre*, Paris, 1945; Mphahlele, Ezekiel, *Down Second Avenue*, London, 1959

[13] Jahn, op. cit.

[14] Firmin, Anténor, *De l'égalité des races humaines*, Paris, 1886, p. 16

[15] Ibid, p. 13

[16] Price, Hannibal, *De la réhabilitation de la race noire par le peuple d'Haïti* Port-au-Prince, 1900, p. 12

[17] Ibid, p. 101
[18] Ibid, p. 640
[19] Césaire, *Cahier*, p. 88
[20] Price-Mars, Jean, *Ainsi parla l'oncle*, Port-au-Prince, 1928, p. 210
[21] Ibid, p. 210
[22] Césaire, *Cahier*
[23] Roumain, *Bois d'ébène*, Port-au-Prince, 1945, p. 6
[24] Niger, Paul, 'Je n'aime pas l'Afrique', in Senghor, op. cit.
[25] Gratiant, Gilbert, 'Sans Mars ni Vénus', Paris, 1944, quoted by Damas, L., in *Poètes d'expression française*, Paris, 1947
[26] Damas, op. cit., p. 159

## Chapter V

## THE THEME OF AFRICA

[1] Thaly, Daniel, 'Le jardin des tropiques', Paris, 1911, p. 7
[2] Brouard, Carl, 'La trouée,' October 1927
[3] Brouard, 'Afrique', *Les Griots*, vol. 2, No. 2, 1939
[4] Casséus, Maurice, 'Tambour racial', *Les Griots*, vol. 4, No. 4, 1939
[5] Laraque, Paul, in St. Louis, Carlos, op. cit., p. 552
[6] Vincent, Sténio, *En posant les jalons*, Port-au-Prince, 1939, pp. 153-4
[7] Bellegarde, Dantès, *Haïti et ses problèmes*, Montreal, 1941, p. 16
[8] Ibid, p. 17
[9] René, Piquion, op. cit.
[10] Labat, *Nouveau voyage aux isles de l'Amérique*, The Hague, 1724, vol. I, p. 149
[11] Roumain, Jacques, Fitts, D., *Anthology of Contemporary Latin American Poetry*, Norfolk, 1947
[12] McKay, op. cit., p. 40
[13] Campbell, George, *First Poems*, Kingston, 1945
[14] Césaire, Aimé, *Présence Africaine*, June–July 1959, pp. 90-1
[15] Palés Matos, op. cit., p. 50
[16] Blanco, Tomás, *Revista Bimestre*, Havana, vol. XXXVIII 1936, p. 40
[17] Ibid, p. 43

## Chapter VI

## REVOLT

[1] Niger, Paul, 'Je n'aime pas l'Afrique'
[2] 'Formes et Couleurs', *Tricinquantenaire de l'Indépendance d'Haïti*, 1954
[3] Brierre, Jean, *Le drapeau de demain*, Port-au-Prince, 1931, p. 28
[4] Bernard, Regnor C., *Nègre*, Port-au-Prince, 1931, p. 12
[5] Damas, *Pigments*, Paris, 1937
[6] Roumain, Jacques, *Bois d'ébène*, Port-au-Prince, 1945, p. 17
[7] Damas, *Poètes d'expression française*, Paris, 1948, p. 15

8 McKay, op. cit., p. 36
9 Rodríguez, Luis Felipe, 'Danza lucumí,' *Revista de Avance*, Havana, February 1930
10 Brierre, Jean, in Senghor, op. cit., p. 127
11 Roumain, Jacques, *Bois d'ébène*, Port-au-Prince, 1946
12 Roumain, Jacques, op. cit.

## Chapter VII

## THE COLOURED WOMAN IN CARIBBEAN POETRY

1 Arredondo, Antonio, *El negro en Cuba*, Havana, 1936, p. 36
2 Ibid, p. 68
3 Louis, Carlos, and Lubin, Maurice, *Panorama de la poésie haïtienne*, Port-au-Prince, 1950, p. 10
4 Morpeau, L., *Anthologie d'un siècle de poésie haïtienne*, Paris, 1925, pp. 95–6
5 St. Louis, op. cit., p. 204
6 Roumer, Émile, *Poèmes d'Haïti et de France*, Paris, 1925
7 Palés Matos, *Tun tun de pasa y grifería*, San Juan, 1950, p. 98
8 St. Louis, op. cit., p. 114
9 Campbell, *First Poems*, Kingston, 1945, p. 15
10 Valbuena, Brione A., and Aquino, L. Hernández, *Nueva poésia de Puerto Rico*, Madrid, 1952, p. 114
11 Damas, *Poètes d'expression française*, Paris, 1947, p. 130
12 Damas, *Pigments*, Paris, 1936
13 McFarlane, J. E. Clare, *Treasury of Jamaican Poetry*, London, 1949, p. 143
14 Garvey, Marcus, *Selections from Poetic Meditations*, New York, 1927
15 Guillén, *El son entero*, Buenos Aires, 1947, p. 32
16 McKay, C., *Selected Poems*, New York, 1953, p. 60
17 Camille, Roussan, *Assaut à la nuit*, Port-au-Prince, 1940
18 The 'negra' or 'mulata' in popular songs collected in countries as far apart as Cuba and the Argentine is invariably described as attractive and desirable, while in the same kind of songs the Negro male is often an object of ridicule and dislike. See Arrom, Julio, 'Presencia del negro en la poesía folklórica americana', in *Certidumbre de América*, Havana, 1959.

## Chapter VIII

## SOCIAL AND PSYCHOLOGICAL PROBLEMS

1 Capécia, Mayotte, *Je suis martiniquaise*, Paris, 1948, p. 202
2 Hopkinson, Slade, *The Four and other Poems*, Barbados, 1954, p. 10
3 Ibid, p. 5

4 Guillén, op. cit., p. 81
5 Ibid, p. 39
6 Bellegarde, Dantès, *La Nation Haïtienne*, Paris, 1938, p. 37
7 Price-Mars, op. cit., p. 3
8 Damas, op. cit., p. 15
9 Cronon, E. D., *Black Moses*, Madison, 1955, pp. 191–2
10 Carr, Ernest A., 'Gan-Gan' in *Caribbean Anthology of Short Stories*, Kingston, 1953
11 Carr, Ernest A. 'Civil Strife' in *Bim*, Vol. III, No. 12, Barbados, 1950
12 Arriví, Francisco, *Vejigantes*, a whole number of *Asomante*, San Juan, 1957
13 Morrison, Hugh P., in *Caribbean Short Stories*, Kingston, 1953
14 Guillén, op. cit., p. 16., in *Motivos de son*, 1930
15 Hernández Catá, Alfonso, *Los frutos ácidos*, Buenos Aires, 1946, p. 103
16 Ibid, p. 102
17 Cotto-Thorner, Guillermo, *Trópico en Manhattan*, San Juan, 1951, p. 150
18 Ibid, p. 49
19 Ibid, p. 68
20 Zobel, Joseph, *La fête à Paris*, Paris, 1953, p. 129
21 Ibid, p. 231
22 Ibid, p. 126
23 Ibid, p. 243
24 Ibid, p. 248
25 Ibid, p. 68
26 Selvon, Samuel, *Lonely Londoners*, London, 1956, pp. 96–7
27 Ibid, p. 170
28 Lamming George, *The Emigrants*, London, 1954, p. 110
29 Ibid, p. 186
30 Ibid, p. 143
31 Ibid, pp. 207–8
32 McKay, Claude, *Banjo*, London, 1929, p. 202

# BIBLIOGRAPHY

*In the case of some Latin American books, the name of the publisher is not known*

Alexis, Jacques Stéphen, *Compère Général Soleil*, Paris, Gallimard, 1955,
    'Du réalisme merveilleux des haïtiens, *Présence Africaine*, Paris, June–
    November 1956
    *Les arbres musiciens*, Paris, Gallimard, 1957
Arredondo, Antonio, *El negro en Cuba*, Havana, 1935
Arriví, Francisco, 'Vejigantes', *Asomante*, San Juan, No. 1 1957
Arrom, José Juan, *Certidumbre de América*, Havana, 1959
Augier, Roy. See Smith, M. G.
Avellaneda, Gertrudis Gómez de, *Sab*, Paris, 1920
Balaguer, Joaquín, *La realidad dominicana*, Buenos Aires, 1947
Ballagas, Emilio, *Mapa de la poesía negra*, Buenos Aires, 1947
Bernard, Regnor C. *Nègres*, Port-au-Prince, 1945
Borges, Jorge Luis, *Cursos y conferencias*, Buenos Aires, 1953
Brierre, Jean, *Le drapeau de demain*, Port-au-Prince, 1931
    *Black Soul*, Havana, 1947
Brouard, Carl, 'Afrique', *Les Griots*, vol. 2, No. 2, Port-au-Prince, 1939
    'Nostalgie', *La Trouée*, Port-au-Prince, October 1927
Cabral, Manuel del, *Doce poemas negros*, Ciudad Trujillo, 1935
    *De este lado del mar*, Ciudad Trujillo, 1949
Calcagnó, Francisco, *Poetas de color*, Havana, 1887
Camille, Roussan, *Assaut à la nuit*, Port-au-Prince, 1940
Campbell, George, *First Poems*, Kingston, 1945
Capécia, Mayotte, *Je suis martiniquaise*, Paris, Editions Corréa, 1948
Carpentier, Alejo, *Ecué-Yamba-O*, Madrid, 1933
Casséus, Maurice, 'Tambour racial', *Les Griots*, vol. 4, No. 4 1939
Césaire, Aimé, *Cahier d'un retour au pays natal*, Editions Bordas, Paris, 1947
    'Les armes miraculeuses', Paris, *Nouvelle Revue française*, 1946
    *Soleil cou coupé*, Paris, Le Prat, 1948
    'Discours sur le colonialisme', Paris, *Présence Africaine*, 1955
    'Culture et colonisation', *Présence Africaine*, 1956
Cinéas, J. B., *Le drame de la terre*, Port-au-Prince, 1933
Coicou, Massillon, *Poésies nationales*, Paris, 1892
Cometta Manzoni, Aida, *El indio en la poesía de América española*, Buenos
    Aires, 1939
Coulthard, G. R., *Survey of British West Indian Literature in Commonwealth
    Pen*, Ithaca, Cornell University Press, 1961
Cotto-Thorner, Guillermo, *Trópico en Manhattan*, San Juan, 1953
Cronon, E. D., *Black Moses*, Madison, University of Wisconsin Press, 1955

Damas, Léon, *Poètes d'expression française*, Paris, Editions du Seuil, 1947
  *Pigments*, Paris, Editions G. L. M., 1937
Dépestre, René, *Minerai noir*, Paris, 1956
Fanon, Frantz, *Peau noire masques blancs*, Paris, Editions du Seuil, 1952
Fernández de Castro, J. A., *Tema negro en la literatura cubana*, Havana, 1943
Firmin, Anténor, *De l'égalité des races humaines*, Paris, Librairie Cotillon, 1885
Fitts, Dudley, *Anthology of Contemporary Latin American Poetry*, Norfolk, New Directions, 1942
Galván, Manuel de Jesús, *Enriquillo* (1882), Bloomington, Indiana University Press, 1954
Garvey, Marcus, *Selections from Poetic Meditations*, New York, A. J. Garvey, 1927
  *The Tragedy of White Injustice*, New York, A. J. Garvey, 1927
  *Philosophy and Opinions*, New York, Universal Publishing House, 1926
Guillén, Nicolás, *El son entero*, Buenos Aires, 1947
Guirao, Ramón, *Orbita de la poesía afrocubana, 1928–37*, Havana, Ucar, Garcia y Cia, 1939
Henríquez Ureña, Max, *Panorama histórico de la literatura dominicana*, Rio de Janeiro, Universidad del Brasila, 1945
Henríquez Ureña, Pedro, *Seis ensayos en busca de nuestra expresion*, Buenos Aires, Biblioteca Argentina de Buenas Ediciones Literias, 1926
Hernández Aquino, L., *Nueva poesía de Puerto Rico*, Madrid, 1952
Hernández Catá, Alfonso, *Los frutos ácidos*, Buenos Aires, 1946
Hopkinson, Slade, *The Four and Other Poems*, Barbados, 1954
Labat, F. Jean-Baptiste, *Nouveau voyage aux isles de l'Amérique*, Paris, Pierre François Giffart, 1722
Lamming, George, *In the Castle of my Skin*, London, Harborough, 1953
  *The Emigrants*, London, Michael Joseph, 1954
  *The Pleasures of Exile*, London, Michael Joseph, 1960
  'The Negro Writer and his World', Paris, *Présence Africaine*, June–November 1956
Lemaître, Georges, *From Cubism to Surrealism in French Literature*, Cambridge, Harvard University Press, 1941
Lubin, Maurice, *Poésies haïtiennes*, Rio de Janeiro, 1956
McFarlane, J. E. Clare, *Treasury of Jamaican Poetry*, University of London Press, 1949
McKay, Claude, *Selected Poems*, New York, 1953
  *Harlem Shadows*, New York, 1922
  *Home to Harlem*, New York, Harper, 1928
  *Banjo*, New York, Harper, 1929
  *Banana Bottom*, New York, Harper, 1933
  *A Long Way from Home*, New York, 1937
Madden, Richard R., *Poems by a Slave of the Island of Cuba Recently Liberated*, London, Thomas Ward, 1840
Manrique Cabrera, Francisco, *Historia de la literatura Puertorriqueña*, New York, 1956
Manzano, Juan Francisco. See Madden, Richard R.

Marinello, Juan, *Poética, ensayos en entusiasmo*, Madrid, 1933
'Sobre una inquietud cubana', *Revista de Avance*, Havana, February 1930
Martí, José, *Obras completas*, Havana, 1953
Masdeu Reyes, Jesús, *La raza triste*, Havana, 1924
Meléndez Concha, 'La novela indianista en Hispanoamericana 1832-1889',
Madrid, *Monografías de la Universidad de Puerto Rico*, 1934
Morpeau, Louis, *Anthologie d'un siècle de poésie haïtienne 1817-1925*, Paris,
Editions Bossard, 1925
Nettleford, Rex, See Smith, M. G.
Ortiz, Fernando, *Hampa afrocubana: los negros brujos*, Madrid, 1906
*Hampa afrocubana: los negros esclavos*, Havana, 1916
*Glosario de afronegrismos*, Havana, 1923
*El engaño de las razas*, Havana, 1945
'Más acerca de una poesía mulata', *Revista Bimestre*, vol. XXXVII,
Havana, 1936
'La poesía mulata', *Revista Bimestre*, vol. XXXIV, Havana, 1934
'Contra los racismos', *Revista de Estudios Afrocubanos*, No. I, Havana,
1937
Palés Matos, Luis, *Tun tun de pasa y grifería*, San Juan (1937?), 1950
*Poesía (1915-1956)*, Introduction by Federico de Onís, San Juan, 1957
Pedroso, Regino, *Antología poética*, Havana, 1939
Pereda Valdés, Ildefono, *Antología de la poesía negra americana*, Montevideo,
1953
Piquion, René, *Langston Hughes: un chant nouveau*, Port-au-Prince, 1945
Portuondo, José Antonio, *El heroísmo intelectual*, Mexico, 1953
*Bosquejo histórico de las letras cubanas*, Havana, 1960
Price, Hannibal, *De la réhabilitation de la race noire*, Port-au-Prince, 1900
Price-Mars, Jean, *Ainsi parla l'oncle*, Port-au-Prince, 1928
Reid, Victor, *New Day*, London, Heinemann, 1950
*The Leopard*, London, Heinemann, 1958
Remos y Rubio, J. J., *Historia de la literatura cubana*, Havana, Cardenas
Compania, 1945
Rodo, José Enrique, *Hombres de América*, Barcelona, Discursos parlamen-
tarios 1920
Roumain, Jacques, *La montagne ensorcelée*, Port-au-Prince, 1931
*Masters of the Dew*, New York, Reynal and Hitchcock, 1947
*Bois d'ébène*, Port-au-Prince, 1946
Roumer, Émile, *Poèmes d'Haïti et de France*, Port-au-Prince, 1925
Sanz y Diaz, José, *La lira negra*, Madrid, 1945
Sartre, Jean-Paul. See Senghor, L. Sédar
Selvon, Samuel, *A Brighter Sun*, London, Alan Wingate, 1952
*Lonely Londoners*, London, Alan Wingate, 1956
Senghor, Léopold Sédar, *Anthologie de la nouvelle poésie nègre et malgache*,
Paris, Presses Universitaires de France, 1948
Smith, M. G., *The Ras Tafari Movement in Kingston, Jamaica*, University Col-
lege of the West Indies, Institute of Social and Economic Research, 1960
St. Louis, Carlos and Lubin, M., *Panorama de la poésie haïtienne*, Port-au-
Prince, 1950

Suárez y Romero, Anselmo, *Francisco*. Prol. *Mario Cabrera Saqui*, Havana,
    Cuadernos de Cultura, 1947
Tardon, Raphaël, *La caldeira*, Paris, Editions Fasquelle, 1949
Ureña de Henríquez, Salomé, *Poesías completas*, Ciudad Trujillo, 1950
Valbuena Brione, A. See L. Hernández Aquino
Varela, J. L., *Ensayos de poesía indígena en Cuba*, Madrid, 1961
Viatte, Auguste, *Histoire littéraire de l'Amérique française des origines à 1950*,
    Paris, Presses Universitaires de France, 1954
Villaverde, Cirilo, *Cecilia Valdés*, Havana, 1941
Vincent, Sténio, *En posant les jalons*, Port-au-Prince, 1939
Vitier, Cintio, *Cincuenta años de poesía cubana 1902-1952*, Havana, Minis-
    terio de Educación, 1952
Zambrana, Antonio, *El negro Francisco; novela de costumbres cubanas*.
    (Preface by J. J. Remos), Havana, 1951
Zobel, Joseph, *La Rue Cases Nègres*, Paris, Jean Froissart, 1950
    'La Fête à Paris', Paris, *Table Ronde*, 1953

# INDEX OF AUTHORS

PRINTED AND BOUND IN ENGLAND BY
HAZELL WATSON AND VINEY LTD
AYLESBURY AND SLOUGH